LABOUR MARKET PROGRAMMES FOR THE POOR IN EUROPE

Labour Market Programmes for the Poor in Europe

Pitfalls, dilemmas and how to avoid them

IDES NICAISE
JOOST BOLLENS
LEN DAWES
SHAHIN LAGHAEI
IVAN THAULOW
MINELLE VERDIÉ
ALAIN WAGNER

Avebury

Aldershot • Brookfield USA • Hong Kong • Singapore • Sydney

Published by
Avebury
Ashgate Publishing Limited
Gower House
Croft Road
Aldershot
Hants GU11 3HR
England

Ashgate Publishing Company
Old Post Road
Brookfield
Vermont 05036
USA

British Library Cataloguing in Publication Data

Nicaise, Ides
    Labour Market Programmes for the Poor in
    Europe: Pitfalls, Dilemmas and How to
    Avoid Them

ISBN 1 85972 181 8

Library of Congress Catalog Card Number: 95-77720

Typeset by
Liesbeth Villa
Higher Institute of Labour Studies (HIVA)
E. Van Evenstraat 2e
B-3000 Leuven

Printed and bound in Great Britain by
Ipswich Book Co. Ltd., Ipswich, Suffolk

Contents

Introduction

1. The context

This is the final report of a research network created within the framework of the European Commission's Third Poverty Programme. In April 1992, the Commission launched a call for transnational research tenders on two themes, one of which dealt with 'contradictions and perverse effects of public policies and practices especially in the area of social policies'. The intention, formulated at a conference on research priorities within the Third Poverty Programme (Bath, October 1990), was to analyse the perverse effects on socially excluded groups of national and European development models on one hand, and the inefficiencies of policies to combat poverty on the other. The topic 'contradictions and perverse effects of social policies' was eventually elaborated in two parallel research projects: this report focuses on the possible 'contradictions and perverse effects' of *labour market policies*. A parallel research project, coordinated by Prof. P. Guidicini, deals with contradictions and perverse effects in *social intervention policies* across Europe. A synthesis article of our book is published in the Journal of European Social Policy (Nicaise e.a., 1995).

2. Aim of the study

There are three primary ways in which the products of economic activity are allocated to citizens or households. Firstly through income from investment; second through direct payments from the State (e.g. social protection) and third through earnings from employment - that is, through the labour market.

The first of these is not of much relevance to the poor; they are unlikely to have a excess disposable income to invest. The second is clearly of relevance, and the rules and definitions of this sphere will be much of our concern; and especially the boundaries between this sphere and the third one. The major point to note here is that social protection, while it is designed to alleviate the worst effects of poverty does not in itself offer ways *out* of poverty. The transition out of poverty can only be made by a transition from dependence on income which flows direct from the state, to earning an income through participation in the labour market.

Therefore, increasing the flow of those who make the transition from living on social protection to living on earnings, and decreasing the flow of those who make the transition from living on earnings to living on social protection, is greatly to the benefit of the State (as well as to the individuals themselves) because it decreases the expenditure levels of the State, and increases its revenue through direct taxation and increased production.

More recent concerns, it has been argued, associated with the relationship between the labour market and poverty are due to changes in the structure of employment increasingly being introduced by employers. Firstly, that transitions from the employed state to the unemployed state are increasing, because of an increase in the proportion of employment which is temporary or short-term rather than permanent. Second, increases in part-time employment (or employment which is low-waged for other reasons) lead to a position in which employment does not necessarily secure freedom from poverty or from the need for some form of, possibly partial, social protection.

Another relevant general point is that the idea of the 'underclass' has led to a debate about whether the issue of poverty is important in a wider sense than just the desire for social justice or for economic efficiency. A view which is put forward, and which may be especially relevant in view of the recent history of Eastern Europe, is that an underclass (but any persistent and large body of poverty however it is described) could be seen as a threat to the stability of economic and social institutions because it raises fundamental questions about the validity of the value systems and practices of the majority culture. This, apart from concerns about poverty, is the focus of concern with the concept of 'social exclusion'.

From this perspective it must be recognised that Europe faces a great threat of increasing unemployment, dualisation and poverty. Not surprisingly, a great variety of programmes have been set up to stimulate reintegration into the labour market, particularly of the most disadvantaged groups.

At the same time, a number of these programmes are yielding rather disappointing results: target groups are not actually being reached, there is a mismatch between intervention strategies and their needs, the impact on the participants' employment probabilities is limited, and in some cases they even lead to new forms of social exclusion.

Of course the purpose of our research is not to 'prove' the ineffectiveness of labour market programmes intended to help the poor in general, but rather to contribute to their improvement by verifying hypotheses with respect to flaws, inconsistencies and unintended side effects on the basis of existing and current evaluation studies. Moreover we hope to point at some 'examples of good practice' where such contradictions and negative side effects have been overcome, and from which other countries could learn. The research should result in a number of policy recommendations with respect to optimal intervention strategies aimed at integrating the poor in the labour market at the national and EU level.

3.   Scope and limitations of this report

Within the area of labour market policies, we will concentrate further on target group-oriented reintegration strategies for unemployed. Macro-economic employment policies are only briefly discussed in the second chapter; they are left out of consideration in the rest of the report, however crucial their role may be in the prevention of poverty.

A further limitation of this report relates to its geographic scope. At the outset, the Commission explicitly requested the project to also deal with poverty and labour market problems of Southern European countries. The involvement of partner institutes from one or more southern member states would have been the best way to guarantee this. However, unforeseen budget constraints did not allow us to extend our network after it had started, so that the more detailed analyses in this report bear only on the five countries involved in the initial network: Belgium, Denmark, France, Luxembourg and the United Kingdom. We hope that this gap will be filled in future research.

Finally, many questions tackled in this research project remain unanswered. Some of them are answered by means of case studies or a cross-national literature study; others have been analysed somewhat more quantitatively; still others remain at the stage of hypothesis formulation. It will appear that many aspects should be explored in greater depth in further research.

Despite all these limitations, we hope that our report will contribute to the public debate on the effectiveness of anti-poverty policy, and eventually, to a better labour market integration of our most deprived citizens. We thank the European Commission for the financial support and for its commitment to this subject.

1 The labour market situation of the poor in Europe

1.1 Who are we talking about ?

Whereas a certain degree of confusion persists at the European level about the terminology concerning poverty and social exclusion (which is inevitable in the light of the diverging cultures and realities across member states), one can observe a growing consensus on a number of descriptive characteristics of the phenomenon. From Townsend's standard definition "Individuals, families and groups in the population can be said to be in poverty when they lack the resources to obtain the type of diet, participate in the activities and have the living conditions and amenities which are customary, or at least widely encouraged, or approved, in the societies to which they belong" (Townsend, 1979, p. 31) we have evolved towards a concept in *which multidimensionality, duration and structural exclusion processes* are seen as essential features. These aspects of poverty or social exclusion have become common knowledge in the European literature.

At the same time, it is generally acknowledged that the groups hit by poverty and social exclusion are heterogeneous. Most authors would agree, to distinguish between at least two main sub-populations that partly overlap each other:
- on the one hand, a population group (consisting mainly of native people) excluded for generations from social progress, afflicted by a cumulation of disadvantages and, above all, by a lack of social power;
- on the other hand, a number of (heterogeneous) groups that have fallen into poverty more recently due to structural changes in society

(migration, unemployment, disintegration of families, ...). Among these groups, too, poverty is characterised by a cumulation of disadvantages, rather than by the incidence of one single social risk.

When it becomes a matter of *operationalizing* this definition, however, then the national context and the zeitgeist begin to play a role. Different approaches are possible.
- First, by identifying recipients of social security, within which we can distinguish categories such as the receivers of the minimum income guarantee (MIG - insofar as this exists), or the long-term unemployed (insofar as they have been identified within the unemployment statistics). The risk is, on the one hand, that the choice of the relevant target groups occurs arbitrarily; on the other hand, it is that social security (including social assistance) does not in itself cover the entire population, so that from the very beginning hidden poverty is left out of consideration.
- Second, by identifying the priority risk groups in the labour market: the long-term unemployed, the recurrent unemployed, people employed in precarious jobs, some migrants, single parent families, young low qualified people, the older unemployed, etc. In view of the subject of this study, such an approach seems advisable, although it is sometimes influenced by coincidental political priorities.
- The third approach makes use of results derived from survey studies, in which the 'poor' are identified in terms of their income (per consumption unit) being below a given threshold. Of course, income in itself is an insufficient measure of prosperity and some groups, such as for instance disabled persons with incomes just exceeding the poverty line, may wrongly be classified as being non-poor. Moreover, many surveys are organised in a way that does not allow them to actually reach the most disadvantaged: ideally, the databases to be used for our purpose should be based on simple face-to-face interviews.

The three approaches are probably complementary. For the general analysis of the position occupied by the poor in the labour market, we propose using the third approach. Accordingly, the population of persons within the active age group who fall below a given poverty line are retained as the relevant target group. In the following chapters, however, we will be forced to use all types of 'indices' based on all three approaches, due to the lack of detailed information on the actual participation of the poor in labour market programmes, the perverse mechanisms in these programmes and their outcomes. This lack of information, especially on the cumulation of disadvantages, will not even be overcome by combining all sources.

1.2 The labour market position of the poor in Europe: a general overview

Intuitively speaking, the link between (new) poverty and unemployment is very straightforward. The rising overall figures on poverty in the EU, from 40 million in 1980 to 51 million in 1990,[1] are generally associated with rising unemployment figures. According to the most recent Eurobarometer survey on the perception of poverty (EC, 1994 - forthcoming), 62% of Europeans think that long-term unemployment is the major factor explaining poverty in the Union. Profile studies of the poor confirm that the risk of poverty is particularly high in households headed by unemployed individuals and moreover, that over time poverty tends to shift from elderly people to younger, unemployed people (see, among others, Cantillon et al., 1994). Panel studies of poor households (Cantillon et al., 1994; Wagner, 1989 and 1993) show that (re)entering employment is a major factor explaining why people escape from poverty.

And yet the relation between poverty and unemployment is not as obvious as is generally believed. In a cross-section analysis of European countries, Gaffikin and Morrissey (1992, p. 34-44) do find a positive correlation between national poverty and unemployment rates, but with some noteworthy exceptions: Belgium, for example, appears to combine a rather high unemployment score with one of the lowest poverty rates within Europe; Greece and Portugal, on the other hand, face high poverty rates while their (official) unemployment statistics are below average. One explanation of the exceptional position of Greece and Portugal may be the existence of hidden unemployment. Another explanation, put forward by the authors, is the unequal level of social protection within the EU.

Additional evidence about the latter determinant is found in the Second annual report of the European Observatory on national anti-poverty policies (Room et al., 1992, p. 72). Out of 10 EU-member states for which statistics were available,[2] 6 appeared to have less than half of their unemployed covered by unemployment insurance or assistance. The coverage ratios ranged from about 5% in Greece to near 90% in Belgium. These figures demonstrate how the causal relationship between unemployment and poverty can be mitigated by social protection measures.

Still, many questions about the labour market situation of the poor, as compared to the non-poor, deserve further investigation. To what degree are the poor in Europe burdened with unemployment ? What is the remaining proportion of working poor ? Why do some unemployed fall into poverty while others do not ? What differences can be observed from country to country ? In the rest of this section an effort is made on the basis of data (that have so far as possible been harmonised) from survey research to answer these questions as far as possible. Taking into account the structural differences between Northern and Southern Europe with respect to the labour market and social security provisions, it should ideally be possible to arrive at a division of the profiles into the following categories:

- unemployed - registered - without benefits
                                      - with benefits
                 - not registered

- employed   - in informal labour market[3]
                 - part time in formal labour market
                 - full time in formal labour market

The comparative statistical material, though, is not simply there for the asking: secondary analyses of existing databases have to be carried out. The fact that most databases are not yet geared to this specific subject and, consequently, will contain insufficiently refined data, constitutes an additional problem. So far the LIS-database (LIS = 'Luxembourg Income Study' - see Smeeding, O'Higgens & Rainwater, 1990) appears to be the best source at the international level for acquiring information about the general profile of the poor and, in particular, about their position in the labour market.[4]

The Luxembourg Income Study is a set of harmonised household surveys from several countries, including many European ones. The basic unit of analysis is the household, while for some years and some countries one can abstract information on the individual level. Apart from some demographic variables, the databases contain information about the level and the source of the different components of household income.

Given the nature of these data, the poverty threshold was defined as an income measure. In what follows, a household (and thus its members) is labelled poor whenever the disposable equivalent income is smaller than one half of the median of the disposable equivalent income of the nation.[5]

Table 1.1 gives an overview of the labour market participation of both poor and non-poor in seven EU-member states.[6] These figures refer to household heads aged 18 to 65 and their partners, if present. This implies that not all of the working-age population is covered. Assuming that all persons between 18 and 65 can be considered as members of the working-age population, two groups will be absent. In the first place, all persons who are neither head nor partner. We presume that this will mainly be young people living with their parents. In the second place, since households whose head is older than 65 are excluded, some spouses younger than 65 will be absent too.

From table 1.1 several conclusions can be drawn:
- For all countries, there is - as expected - a marked difference between the share of working people in the group of the non-poor and the corresponding share in the poor group. However, it is striking that the share of working persons in the poor population is still rather high, especially in Italy and in the UK. Of course, this casts some doubts about the quality and pay of the jobs occupied by the poor. In general, it seems to be the case that among the working poor more respondents have a part time job than among the working non poor. This difference should not be exaggerated, however, except in the case of the Netherlands, where almost one out of two working poor has a part time job.
- With respect to the share of the unemployed, no clear picture emerges, in some countries the share of the unemployed in the non-poor group is larger than this share in the poor group, for other countries it is the other way round. It should be remembered that in some countries, for instance in Italy, youth unemployment is rather important. Since young persons who are neither household head nor spouse are omitted from this sample, youth unemployment will only partially be captured by these figures.
- Since the marked difference between the shares of working persons in both groups is not counterbalanced by the share of unemployed, it can only be counterbalanced by the third category, i.e. those out of the labour force. At first sight, the percentages of this third category are amazingly high, both for the poor and the non poor. Here one should take into account that the figures relate to both the household head and the spouse. Consequently, the proportion of people 'outside the labour force' partly reflects a general problem at the EU-level of low female participation in the labour market - both among the poor and the non-poor. It should be noted, however, that the demarcation be-

tween 'unemployment' on the one hand and 'out of the labour force' on the other hand, is not always clear-cut.[7] Therefore, the unemployment figures in table 1.1 possibly underestimate the real impact of unemployment, whereas the 'out of the labour force' figures possibly are inflated. A typical illustration is the category of single-parent families which may be considered as unemployed or out of the labour force according to national policies with respect to child care facilities. Still, these two reasons do not explain the much *higher* proportion of 'inactive' people *among the poor* as compared to the non-poor: except in the UK and Denmark, the 'inactive' constitute the most important category of poor, followed by the working and - in the last place - the unemployed. This surprising finding inevitably raises the question about the criteria used to define the boundaries of the labour market and more specifically about the 'employability' of the poor. It leads us to the hypothesis that many poor find themselves in such a marginal position vis-à-vis the labour market, that they are no longer considered to be able to contribute productively to the welfare of society. The label 'excluded from the labour market' becomes very significant here. As shown in the following pages, there appears to be a gap between the socially accepted definition of 'unemployed, but still in the labour force' on the one hand and the self-defined wish of the poor to re-enter the labour market on the other.

Table 1.1
Labour force status of household head and spouse, if present

(for Denmark: only head) (households whose head is older than 65 are excluded, for Denmark: pensioners are excluded) (in row percentages)

		Working	Part time		Unemployed	With compensation		Out of the labour force	Missing	Total
		All A	(as % of all working)	(as % of E)	All B	(as % of all unempl.)	(as % of E)	C	D	E=A+B+C+D
Italy	Non Poor	62.58			1.76			35.64	0.03	100
	Poor	43.80			6.24			49.96	0.00	100
UK	Non Poor	70.53	22.30	15.73	1.50			25.29	2.67	100
	Poor	56.76	22.08	12.53	1.11			32.19	9.95	100
Belgium	Non Poor	60.48	6.6	3.99	6.67	94.80	6.33	31.84	1.01	100
	Poor	24.73	8.79	2.17	14.4	98.11	14.13	52.99	7.88	100
Germany	Non Poor	67.76	13.37	9.07	4.25	36.45	1.55	27.44	0.54	100
	Poor	32.89	17.40	5.73	17.24	25.46	4.39	49.17	0.70	100
Netherl.	Non Poor	58.39	14.60	8.53	9.77	23.12	2.26	30.08	1.76	100
	Poor	31.89	45.71	14.58	7.74	20.59	1.59	57.40	2.96	100
Luxemb.	Non Poor	58.76	4.88	2.87	0.00			41.17	0.07	100
	Poor	33.04	10.53	3.48	0.00			66.96	0.00	100
Denmark	Non Poor	92.38			3.14			4.47	0.00	100
	Poor	40.73			32.07			27.19	0.00	100

Source: Luxembourg Income Study and Økonomiministeriet Danmark
The category 'working' includes the insured unemployed in the case of Denmark.

Some complementary information is based on the Europass-project (Deleeck, Van den Bosch and De Lathouwer, 1992). The results, including some regions not covered by LIS, can be found in table 1.2. However, table 1.2 is not completely comparable with table 1.1. Whereas table 1.1 gives the labour market participation rates for both household head and spouse, table 1.2 only gives this information for the household head only. Moreover, in table 1.2 the household heads older than 65 are not excluded, the category retired was excluded instead. The poverty threshold is also slightly different; for both tables the same equivalence scale was used, but table 1.1 is based on the median, whereas table 1.2 is based on the average household income.

Table 1.2
Labour force status of household head
(households whose head is retired are excluded) (in row percentages)

		Em-ployed	Unem-ployed	Sick	Other	Total
Belgium	Non poor	87.90	6.05	4.28	1.77	100
(1985)	Poor	41.91	35.01	8.19	14.89	100
Ireland	Non poor	73.33	6.27	6.53	13.86	100
(1987)	Poor	42.84	38.89	9.12	9.15	100
Lorraine	Non poor	88.2	3.63	2.61	5.55	100
(1986)	Poor	50.28	19.72	6.06	23.94	100
Netherl.	Non poor	81.92	5.00	7.90	5.18	100
(1986)	Poor	49.38	13.31	9.65	27.67	100
Luxemb.	Non poor	77.73	0.54	5.92	15.88	100
(1986)	Poor	54.67	4.55	17.43	23.35	100
Catalonia	Non poor	88.14	3.53	3.45	4.87	100
(1988)	Poor	55.85	17.42	15.18	11.54	100
Greece	Non poor	92.16	1.14	0.00	6.70	100
(1988)	Poor	90.73	2.71	0.00	6.56	100

Source: Deleeck e.a. (1992), p. 142-143 and own calculations

Here the absence of the spouse changes the picture to some extent. The shares of employed and unemployed persons increase, whereas the importance of 'out of the labour force' declines, as compared with table

1.1. The category 'out of the labour market' is no longer predominant. On the other hand, the difference between the poor and the non-poor with regard to unemployment becomes more pronounced. But still in most countries studied the share of the 'inactive' among the poor household heads appears to be much higher than that of the unemployed. Is this genuine inactivity, or hidden unemployment?

1.3 The labour market situation of the poor in Belgium: a more detailed illustration

No matter how necessary and informative large-scale statistical studies may be, they do elicit a need for complementary data from small-scale, more detailed research. By way of illustration, we therefore cite the results of a survey of the labour market situation of poor people in Belgium (spring 1994). A random sample of 273 adults living in poverty was questioned, via intermediaries from the Movement ATD-Fourth World and similar organisations.[8] Only people 'who want to work and can work' were included in the sample. Consequently, the category 'out of the labour market' is theoretically excluded a priori. However, we shall see that many persons would be classified as such in large-scale surveys using administrative definitions of the respondents' labour market situation.

If we look first of all at the *employment rate*, the following picture emerges: 62.3% of them were entirely without work. In addition, another 15.8% were employed part-time,[9] while approximately 22% were working full-time.

It must also be noted that there are all kinds of grey areas on the fringes of 'complete unemployment': how does one classify, for example, an unemployed person who works voluntarily for an association, a disabled person who makes a little bit of extra cash delivering newspapers, or an unemployed person who occasionally moonlights? Occasional extra earnings are generally not included in our figures.

Of those from the sample who were entirely without work, only one in two (31% of the overall sample) was drawing normal unemployment benefits. A definition of 'unemployment' based on the social security status of the individual would therefore record a 'full unemployment level' of 31% instead of 62%. Using this criterion, the remainder would perhaps fall within the category of 'outside the labour market'.

Nonetheless, the intermediaries involved define the remainder as 'job-seekers'. These people often live on a sickness or disability benefit (12.5% of the total sample) or on income support (minimum income guarantee = MIG - 15%), or they have no income at all (4.5%). One can suppose that in other European countries, disabled people looking for work are not classed as 'unemployed' either, which increases their marginalisation from the labour market. In Belgium, the same largely applies to those on income support, where only a fraction are registered as job-seekers with the employment offices.

The survey results given therefore show, despite the limited scope of the sample, that exclusion from the labour market does not necessarily coincide with the official concept of 'unemployment'. The status of a great many people is such that they are generally located 'outside the labour market', or at least 'in the margin' of it, even if they are actually looking for work.

The survey also illustrates the *poor social protection* given to the group in question. If minimum income recipients and those with no income are combined, it is evident that one third of those (fully or partially) unemployed get no help from conventional social security systems. This phenomenon is typical of continental European social security systems, where the principle of 'contribute first, benefit later' is heavily predominant. A great many marginal workers in fact fall by the wayside because they were not initially able to contribute through a stable job, so as to be eligible for social security benefits later.

One striking aspect of poor social protection relates to sickness and disability insurance. The survey reveals, among other things, the weak state of health of many poor people. Approximately 40% of them had problems[10] in this area, even leaving out of the survey those who were totally unable to work. Among those in the sample who were partially fit for work, only one in three received a disability benefit; one in five (19%) had neither income from employment nor a replacement income.

Table 1.3
Labour market situation of a sample of poor people
in Belgium, March 1994

	Full-time employed		Part-time employed		Totally inactive		Total[2]	
	N	%[1]	N	%	N	%	N	%
Employment status	60	22	42	15.5	-	-	102	37.5
standard[3]	24	9	17	6	-	-	41	15
sheltered work-shop	15	5.5	-	-	-	-	15	5.5
employment project	14	5	10	4	-	-	24	9
no stat./moonl.	7	2.5	15	5.5	-	-	22	8
Unemployment status	-	-	42	15.5	171	63	213	78
unempl. benefit	-	-	6	2	84	31	90	33
sickn./disab. ben.	-	-	7	2.5	34	12.5	41	15
MIG	-	-	6	2	40	15	46	17
no repl. inc.	-	-	23	8.5	12	4.5	35	13
Total	60	22	42	15.5	171	63	273	100

[1] As % of the total sample (273 persons).

[2] Note: the figures in these columns are partially overlapping: part-time unemployed = part-time employed.

[3] 'Standard employment' here means a normal employment contract (irrespective of length, possibly temporary) or independent status, with social security protection, not in an absorption programme.

So far, we have been primarily concerned with unemployment and the social security status of poor people. The reverse of this is the labour situation of those who work, both full-time and part-time.

Barely one in three of those employed works full-time in a regular job and is in order with social security payments. The rest either work part-time, in temporary jobs, in a sheltered workshop or employment project (usually in an unemployment reduction programme), or they have neither status nor social security cover.

It should be noted that precarious employment conditions are not the exclusive preserve of the private, open labour market. For want of resources, a great many non-profit-making initiatives provide work for the underprivileged in an 'unemployment absorption status' and as 'volunteers' (sometimes under pressure) while the latter retain their benefits or even moonlight. A typical problem relates to those working in sheltered workshops: of 16 people recorded as such in our sample, only 5 had a disability benefit. As wages in the Belgian sheltered workshops are still considered as a supplement to disability pensions, they are set far below the legal minimum wage. This implies that some non-handicapped people employed in sheltered workshops stay below the poverty line while working full-time.

Approximately three-quarters of the jobs held by our respondents are in the private services sector, particularly in personal services. The hotel and catering sector and the building sector also employ a considerable number of underprivileged people. The most common jobs are (in order of occurrence): cleaning lady or home help, scrap metal dealer, gardener, building worker, handyman, barman or kitchen worker.

The Belgian study is most probably not representative of other European countries. In Southern Europe especially the social security situation of poor people can be expected to be much weaker and, consequently, a lot more part-time, informal work will be revealed. However, information about this is extremely patchy. Even rough statistics on the labour market position of poor people in Southern European member states is largely non-existent. Unfortunately, the limited scope of this study did not enable us to carry out much investigative work into this aspect.

1.4 Conclusion

On the whole, three main conclusions can be drawn from the above analysis.

1. Poor people are often marginalised from the labour market to such an extent that they are treated as 'outside the labour market' rather than as job-seekers. This of course makes their integration all the more difficult. This issue will be examined in greater detail in chapter 3 (barriers to entry).

2. We must not forget that a great many poor people are economically active in spite of everything, albeit in part-time and highly precarious statutes. Therefore, policy in this respect must be aimed not just

at creating new jobs, but also at improving the quality of work in certain sectors. But, as stated earlier, this subject falls beyond the scope of this report.

3. The causal link between unemployment and poverty can to some extent be cut through by adequate social protection systems: sufficiently high unemployment benefits and a long-term protection where necessary. Obviously, this is a strategy curing the symptoms rather than the causes of poverty. The rest of this report will therefore be focused on (re)integration strategies - although it will become evident very soon that labour market reintegration is not in contradiction with social protection.

Notes

1 Number of European inhabitants with equivalent income below 50% of the national average - EU-12, Eurostat estimates.

2 UK and Portugal are missing.

3 By informal employment we understand different kinds of a-typical jobs, mainly in the services' sector, that are not regulated nor protected by work legislations and social security. It does not necessarily coincide with 'black work': it can as well consist of self-employment in marginal activities and in barter activities.

4 The Europass-project, too (Deleeck, Van den Bosch and de Lathouwer, 1992), contains some comparative data for five countries (or at least, regions). Unfortunately, no secondary analysis can be done of the Europass data because the data banks have not been merged. It will not yet be possible for our study to utilize the new 'Europanel' project of Eurostat because it is still in the pilot phase.

5 For more details, see appendix.

6 Figures for Denmark, although not in LIS, are also included in table 1.1, since they are derived using an identical poverty threshold.

7 In the case of Luxembourg, the (small) group of unemployed is in fact included in the category 'out of the labour market'.

8 The 'poor' selection criterion was left entirely to the contact persons of the organisation in question. Although no income limit was assumed at all here, we believe that the random sample therefore provides a more representative picture of genuine, multi-faceted poverty. The contact persons in question do after all receive a continuing training in poverty within the ATD-Fourth World Movement, which makes them better able to estimate the overall situation of one person than would be possible using statistical criteria. Youngsters were included insofar as they have left full-time education.

9 Part-time or interim workers.

10 Health problems were defined as physical, psychic or mental deficiencies that might hamper a normal working life.

2 Poverty and labour market policy: An overview

2.1 Introduction

It is obviously not our intention to make an exhaustive evaluation of all labour market programmes in Europe. What we are endeavouring to achieve is that our report should be more or less representative of the most important types of labour market policy relating to combating poverty in the countries under study - and perhaps indirectly, of more general strategies throughout Europe. In a first step, a broad overview is given of the main strategies followed in the European Union; in a second step, we try to classify the most relevant programmes in the five countries under study into a common framework. The last section of this chapter gives an overview of the discussion on pitfalls and dilemmas that will be discussed in the next chapters.

2.2 General tendencies in Europe

In all the countries of the EU, substantial means are devoted to labour market policy. In table 2.1, public expenditures on, and the number of participants in active labour market policy measures can be found for all countries of the European Union. It should be noted that this table contains information for both specific and general programmes.

Table 2.1
Public expenditure and participants inflows in labour market programmes, EU-12

		Vocational training (1)	Recruitment services (2)	Employment subsidies (3)	Enterprise allowance (4)	Orientation guidance (5)
B 91	% GDP	0.14	-	0.55	-	0.19
	% lab. force	1.80	-	3.10	-	
DK 92	% GDP	0.53	-	0.28	0.11	0.11
DK 91	% lab. force	2.40	-	1.90	0.20	
F 91	% GDP	0.38	0.14	0.09	0.02	0.13
	% lab. force	n.a.	1.80	1.10	0.20	
GER 92	% GDP	0.61	0.01	0.52	-	0.24
	% lab. force	n.a.	0.2	1.50	0.10	
GR 92	% GDP	0.05	0.03	0.06	0.03	0.07
	% lab. force	0.20	0.30	0.30	0.20	
IR 91	% GDP	0.62	0.15	0.27	0.02	0.14
	% lab. force	4.00	0.70	1.40	0.10	
IT 88	% GDP	0.29	0.43	-	-	0.08
	% lab. force	n.a.	n.a.	n.a.	n.a.	
LUX 91	% GDP	0.08	0.05	0.02	-	0.04
	% lab. force	n.a.	n.a.	n.a.	n.a.	

Table 2.1

Public expenditure and participants inflows in labour market programmes, EU-12 (continued)

		Vocational training (1)	Recruitment services (2)	Employment subsidies (3)	Enterprise allowance (4)	Orientation guidance (5)
NL 92	% GDP	0.21	0.04	0.11	-	0.15
	% lab. force	1.80	0.60	0.40	-	
PORT 92	% GDP	0.15	0.29	0.02	0.02	0.09
	% lab. force	1.40	1.60	0.20	0.20	
SP 92	% GDP	0.12	-	0.20	0.12	0.11
SP 90	% lab. force	0.15	-	4.90	0.50	
UK 92/93	% GDP	0.16	0.18	-	0.02	0.17
	% lab. force	0.90	0.70	-	0.10	

-: nil or small

(1) Training for unemployed adults and those at risk, measures for unemployed and disadvantaged youth.
(2) Support of apprenticeship and related forms of youth training.
(3) Subsidies to regular employment in private sector and direct job creation.
(4) Support of unemployed persons starting enterprises.
(5) Placement, counselling and vocational guidance, job-search courses, support of geographic mobility and administration costs of labour market agencies.

Source: OECD (1993), Employment Outlook 1993

By and large *training* for job seekers is the most important policy measure. It has long been considered everywhere as a prime implement for combating unemployment and long-term unemployment, and more generally speaking as a means of combating social exclusion. Taking steps to provide those out of work with training and qualifications may not by itself be enough to reduce unemployment, but it does offer several advantages.

- As a result of the industrial changes and the rise in the rate of unemployment, it has become increasingly clear that less qualified workers tend to be excluded from the labour market more often, so raising their level of skills is tantamount to increasing their chances of (re)integration into the labour market.
- The very fact of taking part in a qualification-based programme prevents job-seekers from becoming accustomed to long periods of inactivity, as this is recognised as being detrimental to the moral, health and motivation of those looking for work.
- A mismatch is seen to exist between the qualifications of those seeking jobs and the skills required for the jobs on offer. As a result of the structural changes throughout Europe, the demand for a qualified labour force becomes more and more prevalent, whereas non-qualified labour becomes redundant. Training is moreover seen as an effective instrument to reduce social and regional inequality.

In comparing the relative weight of training with that of other labour market strategies, it is clear that not all countries use the same *policy-mix*. On the whole, there seems to be a positive correlation between the expenditures on vocational training for the unemployed on the one hand and the expenditures on direct employment on the other hand, the former in general being higher than the latter. Some noteworthy exceptions are Belgium, where the expenditures on direct employment measures are far more important than the training expenditures, and the UK, Portugal and Italy, where direct employment expenditures is a minor fraction of the training expenditures. The expenditures on orientation and guidance are quite comparable across countries, whereas expenditures on enterprise allowances, i.e. support for unemployed persons starting an enterprise, differ widely.

In terms of *trends*, a first well-known fact is the increasing proportion of spending in most parts of Europe on active measures, especially on training and youth measures (OECD, 1992). This tendency is not merely confined to a quantitative expansion of traditional training and employment expenditures, it also involves the development of new strategies. During the last years a new type of programme is emerging in several countries, to wit an 'umbrella' type programme which comprises various optional measures including counselling and guidance, training, job-search training and placement and which tries go give an individual approach, tailored towards the needs of each individual job-seeker - mostly of the long-term unemployed. Examples of this approach are the 'Weer-Werk' programme and the 'Guidance Plan' in Belgium, 'Objectif 900 000' in France, 'Restart' in the UK and the 'Individual Action Plan' in Denmark.

As far as these programmes really provide for intensive support to disadvantaged unemployed, they are undoubtedly redistributing employment opportunities. They become somewhat double-edged, however, in that some of the recent programmes have a *mandatory* nature and are, at the same time, used to test the availability of the beneficiaries for the labour market. In this way, they also carry with them a danger of generating additional risks of exclusion for those who do not follow the 'rules of the game properly'; and they might undermine the working conditions in the regular labour market by exerting pressure on the long-term unemployed and other disadvantaged groups to accept low-quality jobs.

This pressure is most visible in social assistance and youth schemes, where mandatory participation in training or work programmes is often becoming a condition of access to social assistance benefits. Examples are found in the MIG-schemes of the five countries studied here (Belgium, Denmark, France, Luxembourg, UK), as well as in Spain; examples of mandatory youth schemes are found in the UK (Youth Training), Denmark and the Netherlands. Most of these mandatory programmes should not be labelled as workfare, in the sense of mandatory work in return for welfare benefits. Strictly speaking, this is only the case for the Danish 'job offer in the public sector'-programme. The pros and cons of mandatory programmes in terms of equity and efficiency deserve a closer analysis. Particular attention will be devoted to this type of programmes in chapter 4.

Next to this development, in some countries the so-called *'social economy'* sector (social cooperatives, insertion enterprises, ...) is becoming an important new instrument of labour market policy. These social economy initiatives, which are rather heterogeneous, have some characteristics in common: they are oriented towards the market, i.e. they produce services and goods for the market, but profit making is not the first goal, the employment of vulnerable groups is given priority instead. Nevertheless, their economic viability and links with the regular labour market remain major questions of concern for policy makers and field workers. This problem will be tackled in chapter 6 (segmentation).

2.3 Relevant labour market programmes in the five countries studied

As stated earlier, the analysis will be confined to programmes relating to the (re)integration of unemployed people into the regular labour market, leaving aside, for example, preventive actions to maintain jobs, or policies focused on the upgrading and regulation of informal labour. Within the (re)integration strategies, a further distinction can be made between general and selective labour market programmes.
- The *general* labour market programmes are relevant in this framework as far as the poor as a target group fall within the radius of action of general policy.
- Of the *selective* programmes, only those that are relevant for the poor will be studied.

The labour market programmes selected according to these criteria are classified in table 2.2 according to a modified OECD typology (prevocational training, vocational training, recruitment incentives, direct employment in absorption programmes, social economy initiatives, aid for beginning self-employed persons, orientation and guidance, and possibly mixed programmes). A provisional overview of such programmes for the member states involved in the network is to be found in table 2.2.

Table 2.2
Overview of relevant labour market programmes

Type of programme		Provision / measure	Target group	Comment
Prevocational education and training	B	• COISP (FOREM)	Low-qualified 15 - 18 y.	
		• Brugprojecten	Disadvantaged 'Risk groups'	
		• Some non-profit initiatives		
		• 0.25 (Employment Fund)		
	DK	• Prevocational education	MIG	
		• Special activation courses	MIG, < 25 y.	
		• Project 'use for everybody'	MIG	Expired
		• Special educational training	Insured + MIG	Activation offer to LTU
	LUX	• CFPC (Centres pour la Formation Professionnelle Continue)	Unemployed and MIG	Initiation and orientation course
	UK	• Youth Training	< 25 y.	Since 1983 about 3.1 million people
	F	• Stage d'insertion	MIG	
		• Crédit-Formation Individualisé	Youngsters	
Vocational training	B	• Training courses VDAB / FOREM	General 'Risk-groups'	
		• 0.25 sectoral initiatives		
	DK	• Job training in public sector	Insured + MIG	Usually for LTU 2-4 weeks
		• AMU courses	Manual worker	

Note: MIG = minimum income guarantee receivers

Table 2.2
Overview of relevant labour market programmes (continued)

Type of programme		Provision / measure	Target group	Comment
Vocational training	LUX	• Primes d'orientation • Formation des adultes	< 30 y. Employed adults	
	UK	• Training for work	> 6 m. unempl., priority for some disadvantaged groups	Well established
	F	• PAQUE • Actions d'Insertion et de Formation • Stages Fonds Nat. pour l'emploi	< 25 y Adult unemp. Adult unemp.	
Recruitment incentives	B	• Programme-law 1988 • RD 495 • 0.25 • Stage des jeunes • PRIME • Plus	LTU - other 15 - 25 y. 'Risk-group' < 30 y. LTU Hard to place unemployed	Apprenticeships Employment subsidy
	DK	• Job training in private sector	Insured + MIG	Relatively good employment

Note: MIG = minimum income guarantee receivers

Table 2.2

Overview of relevant labour market programmes (continued)

Type of programme		Provision / measure	Target group	Comment
Recruitment incentives	LUX	• Recr. incentive	LTU (> 15 m.), hard to place u.	
		• Stages de préparation en entreprise		
		• Aides à la mobilité géographique		
		• Aide au réemploi		
		• Law 23 July 1993		Repayment social contributions, 2 to 7 m., private sector
	UK	• Workstart	> 6 m. unempl.	New, pilot scheme
	F	• Contrats de Retour à l'Emploi		
		• EXO-jeunes	Young	
		• Contrat Emploi-Solidarité	MIG	
		• Entreprises d'Insertion		
Direct employment	B	• Troisième Circuit du Travail	LTU	
		• Agents Contractuels Subventionnés (ACS)	LTU	
Direct employment	DK	• Special Job Training	Insured + MIG	Hard to place u.

Note: MIG = minimum income guarantee receivers

Table 2.2
Overview of relevant labour market programmes (continued)

Type of programme		Provision / measure	Target group	Comment
	LUX	• Contrat stage-initiation	Unempl, < 30 y.	Public or social sector
		• Auxiliaires temporaires	< 30 y.	
		• Travaux extraordinaires d'intérêt général		
		• Affectation temporaire d'insertion	MIG ?	
		• Stage en entreprise privée	MIG ?	
	UK	• Community Action	LTU (> 12 m.)	
		• Work Trials	> 6 m. unempl., priority for some disadvantaged groups	
	F	• CES (contrats emploi-solidarité)	MIG	
'Social Economy' initiatives	B	• 'Social workshops'	Most hard to place	
		• 'Integration enterprises'	Hard to place unempl.	
		• Entreprise d'apprentissage profes-sionnel	Youngsters, MIG	
	LUX	• Affectation temporaire d'insertion	MIG	
	UK	• Community Business (Scotld)	LTU, locals	
		• Task Force, City Challenge	Inhabitants disadvan-taged localities	

Note: MIG = minimum income guarantee receivers

Table 2.2
Overview of relevant labour market programmes (continued)

Type of programme		Provision / measure	Target group	Comment
'Social Economy' initiatives	F	• Associations intermédiaires	Hard to place unempl.	
		• Régies de quartier		
		• Entreprise d'Insertion	Hard to place unempl.	
Enterprise allowance schemes	B	• Prêt-chômeur	General	
	DK	• Enterprise allowance	MIG	Small scale
		• Enterprise allowance	Insured	Pos. employm. effect
	LUX	• Enterprise allowance	Insured unempl.	
	UK	• Business Start Up	> 6 m. unempl., priority for some disadvantaged groups	Creaming-off is evident
	F	• Enterprise allowance	General	
Orientation and guidance	B	• Contrat d'intégration	MIG	
		• Jobclub	General	
		• Plan d'accompagnement	Insured unem, > 9m., under 45 y.	
		• Weer-werk	LTU, Flanders	

Note: MIG = minimum income guarantee receivers

Table 2.2
Overview of relevant labour market programmes (continued)

Type of programme		Provision / measure	Target group	Comment
Orientation and guidance	DK	• Guidance course	Insured	Offer prior to activation
		• Youth guidance	MIG < 25 y.	Inspiration + orientation
		• Municipal guidance courses	MIG	Introductory
		• Individual action plan	Insured + MIG	Totally new
	LUX	• Action locale pour jeunes	Youngsters with difficulties	
		• Actions des initiatives locales pour l'emploi		Private organisations
	UK	• Jobclubs	> 6 m. unempl., priority for some disadvantaged groups	Well-liked and cost-effective
		• Job Plan Workshops	> 12 m. unempl.	Mandatory, mostly (benefit sanction)
		• Restart Course	> 24 m. unempl.	Mandatory, mostly (benefit sanction)
		• Job Search Seminars	> 3 m. unempl., priority for some disadvantaged groups	Jobclub for short term unemployed
	F	• Objectif 900 000	LTU	
		• Contrat d'insertion	MIG	
		• Modules d'Accueil et d'Orientation		

Note: MIG = minimum income guarantee receivers

Table 2.2
Overview of relevant labour market programmes (continued)

Type of programme		Provision / measure	Target group	Comment
Mixed programmes	B	• Weer-Werk	LTU	New ideas (in '94, '95 projects in humanit. & cultural areas)
		• Emploi et formation pour les défavorisés	MIG	
	DK	• Experimental projects	Insured + MIG	
		• Rehabilitation programme	All	Persons with reduced work capacity
	UK	• Job Interview Guarantee	> 6 m. unempl., priority for some disadvantaged groups	

Note: MIG = minimum income guarantee receivers

2.4 Contradictions and perverse effects: a general discussion

The 'contradictions and perverse effects' may be classified into two basic categories:
- contradictions between 'selective' policies in favour of specific (disadvantaged) target groups on the one hand and the general, macro-economic policies on the other;
- contradictions and perverse effects within (selective) reinsertion programmes targeted towards specific risk groups.

The former type of contradictions will be discussed at length in what follows, whereas the latter will be tackled more briefly, as they will be developed more extensively in the following chapters.

2.4.1 Contradictions between selective and general policies

To acknowledge that poverty is a structural problem, is to call into question the very foundations of our society. From a European labour market perspective, poverty is clearly related to Europe's dualistic grown strategy, the free market economy and the dominant role of capital and technology in it. Four examples of contradiction between the macro-economic policy and the problem of integrating the poor into the labour market are discussed below.

Europe's dualistic growth strategy

Great efforts are being made to improve the employment opportunities of disadvantaged groups, while at the same time we are observing growing factor price distortions that are destroying employment. It appears as if Europe has opted for a 'dualistic', labour saving growth path, combining high productivity and high wages with high unemployment, ... and high levels of social protection. Some would argue that this is the result of exogenous technological and socio-demographic factors, rather than a result of deliberate political choices. However, a comparison with other economic powers shows that the European growth path has its own particular features. Between 1970 and 1991, the GDP of the European Union rose by 73.4%, which is about the same growth figure as in the USA (74.8%). Over the same time span, aggregate employment in Europe rose by no more than 6.1%, compared to 41.1% in the USA. The difference is explained by a much higher productivity growth in the EU, boosted by wage pressures, and accompanied by a steady rise in unemployment.

The heavy tax burden on (low) wages

Part of the upward wage pressure in Europe is to be explained by factor price distortions between labour and other factors of production,
due to their unequal *fiscal and parafiscal treatment*. The harmonisation of
taxes on interests at a moderate level and the subsidisation of capital
investments in depressed regions have gone together with a strong increase in the fiscal and parafiscal burden on wages and extreme pressures on labour productivity growth, which inevitably lead to a growth
in unemployment. This paradox has been recognised in publications of
the EC, like the Commission's White Paper (1994) and its report on 'Social protection in Europe' (1994). The net wage of an unmarried unskilled worker in Europe averages 52% of his/her gross salary cost; between 1970 and 1991, the direct tax burden on wages has increased by
40%, that is twice as much as in the USA. Of course, part of this tax
burden is compensated by social transfers in periods of inactivity, but
the question is often posed whether the burden could be shifted to
other factors of production, in order to avoid perverse effects on employment. This has become one of the main options of the White Paper
for the next decade.

A related issue concerns the distribution of social contributions between high and low wages. The White Paper mentions that in eight of
the present 12 EU-member states, these levies are *regressive*, i.e. relatively higher for low than for high wages. It suggests lowering the
parafiscal burden especially on the lowest wages and to compensate
this by energy taxes and also, possibly, a higher taxation of capital income.

The EMU and its implications for the poor

All things considered, the economic and monetary convergence does
exact its toll, even if in the longer term it can lead to a higher level of
prosperity and more employment. In the first place, in a number of
member states the national budgets are under great pressure, which
indirectly affects social policy and, thus, poverty. In the second place,
there is the heightened competition, due to which sectors and activities
with a high concentration of unskilled labour, particularly in periph-
eral regions, will inevitably have to cut back and this means an increasing risk of 'social dumping'. Gaffikin and Morrissey (1992) review a
number of studies (Grahl and Teague, 1990; Cutler, 1989; Rajan, 1990)
that are quite sceptical about the employment prospects of the single
market, unless it is accompanied by specific interventions to improve

the economic and social cohesion. The reform and extension of the structural funds, the creation of the cohesion fund and more recently, the new employment strategy advocated in the Commission's White Paper, are steps in this direction; whether the latter will be fully implemented and will provide for a sufficient impulse remains an open question.

Active labour market strategies: activating labour supply ?

Unemployment is basically a situation of excess supply (and/or depressed demand) in labour markets. During the 1980s, many countries tried to restore the equilibrium by reducing labour supply: early retirement and career interruption schemes were launched, part-time employment was stimulated. The traditional Keynesian recipe, demand stimulation, had become obsolete, as it led to structural budget deficits, debt accumulation, and consequently, increasing interest rates and inflation. The Keynesian theory appeared unable to cope with the new problem of stagflation.

But it became clear very soon that the reduction of labour supply basically triggered the same mechanisms as demand stimulation: the 'passive labour policies'[1] turned out very costly as well, and were finally disqualified by orthodox neo-classical labour economics (Layard, Nickel and Jackman, 1991; Gaffikin and Morrissey, 1992). This explains why at present a reverse strategy is being adopted: labour supply is stimulated by 'active measures' instead of reduced. The minimum ages for early retirement are being increased, and in some countries part-time employment is no longer really being encouraged, because of their high cost to the government. (For example, in Belgium jobs of less than 13 hours/week are simply forbidden, employers hiring part-time unemployed people have to pay extra social security contributions, and unemployment benefits for these people have been reduced.) In many countries, as we have seen, an increasing pressure is exerted on long-term unemployed (LTU) to accept lower-standard jobs, the most typical example being the British Job start scheme, which provides for allowances to LTU who 'accept' a job within 3 months. The underlying philosophy of this new strategy is that simultaneous growth stimulation and the fight against inflation can only be achieved through supply-stimulating measures. Indeed, when supply rises, economic transactions tend to increase and prices tend to fall.

Whereas this argument seems logical concerning the markets for goods and services, it is less straightforward for labour markets, which

---

are already characterised by a situation of excess supply. Stimulating labour supply by means of active labour market policies may thus indirectly *enhance* unemployment rates and poverty. The poor may be particularly vulnerable to these measures, as they often occupy marginal and part-time jobs.

The advocates of active labour market policy will reply that it does not only aim to increase labour supply, but rather to increase its flexibility. LTU and low-skilled job-seekers should be retrained and geared towards the new, dynamic sectors of the economy, in order to avoid rigidities and wage inflation, and to raise their productivity; contracts should be made more flexible to lower the fixed costs of labour; etc. (Andersen, 1992). To some extent these strategies are quite legitimate, given the handicap of high labour costs in Europe, mentioned above. But even without boosting labour supply, such measures would not fundamentally resolve the problem of unemployment; they are more effective as a means to combat inflation and to redistribute (un)employment than as employment creation strategies. In some extreme cases, they may even lead to a downgrading of labour conditions in precarious jobs, and thus to more poverty.[2]

This failure of active labour market strategies to yield the expected employment creation effects has been recognised by the OECD in its Employment Outlook 1993 (p. 46-53). In a cross-section analysis of 21 countries over the period 1985-1990, the macro-economic impact of active labour market policies on employment was estimated after controlling for other factors such as growth of GDP and wages, by means of regression analysis. Paradoxically, employment growth turned out to be *negatively* (instead of positively) related to growth in expenditure on active measures. In other words, countries raising their expenditures on active measures saw their unemployment grow faster (or diminish less) than other countries. The paradox can only be understood by inverting the causal relation: as unemployment rose, governments reacted by spending more on labour market measures. But anyhow, the results demonstrate the ineffectiveness of active measures in reducing unemployment. Similar estimates of their influence on *wage* levels indicated that in most countries (but far from all), active labour market measures tend to 'facilitate wage moderation'. But apparently, not to an extent that would affect employment growth substantially.

Because of the broad reach of such issues and the limited scope of our study, it was decided not to develop in greater detail the issues raised above about the relation between poverty and *macro-economic* labour market issues. Nevertheless, it seemed necessary to mention these problems in order to place the remaining issues in a broader context. From the discussion so far we need to remember that the general macro-economic context in Europe is rather one of a deep structural crisis that produces poverty and social exclusion, even if it goes in tandem with a high living standard of the majority of the population. High wage costs, excessive taxation of labour, tight monetary policies, and the absence of effective macro-economic strategies to cope with unemployment determine the context within which programmes are developed to give disadvantaged groups new chances of (temporary) reintegration. Is this 'mopping with open taps'? In any case, as the problem seems to be one of uneven distribution and dualism rather than economic recession, it seems worthwhile to examine whether more solidaristic solutions, e.g. a stronger commitment to redistribute labour (together with income and social security contributions), would offer a valuable alternative.

2.4.2 Pitfalls and dilemmas within (targeted and general) reinsertion programmes

Barriers to entry (chapter 3)

Many labour market programmes, even for disadvantaged groups, are closely linked with the social security system, being focused on 'officially registered' unemployed, thus excluding social assistance beneficiaries. Some groups living in relative poverty are not even recognised as being part of the labour force.

Mismatches between provisions and needs (chapter 4)

The apparent demotivation of the long-term unemployed vis-à-vis training offers can sometimes be explained by *mismatches between the content of the schemes and their needs*. For many of them, work is a first priority, whereas training is offered to them without any guarantee of work after the scheme. Other mismatches relate to the material and psychological constraints that prevent candidates from participating.

Equity - efficiency dilemmas (chapter 5)

Employment agencies in charge of the execution of programmes in favour of disadvantaged groups may be afraid of losing their credibility among employers by using 'adverse selection criteria'. A natural reaction is to 'cream off' the target groups so as to obtain the best placement results. Sometimes the selection criteria of employment agencies take very subtle, perhaps even 'unconscious' forms.

Dead end provisions, stigma effects and carousels (chapter 6)

The reluctance of some employment agencies to take on the burden of the least employable groups has urged non-governmental organisations to set up specific projects for these people. However, these NGO's have less technical and economic know-how, unstable subsidies and less equipment to organise training, even if they are more familiar with the target groups. Consequently, the learning effects and placement results of these projects are sometimes poor.

Stigma effects are sometimes encountered in 'alternative' projects, in which more or less permanently subsidised, low-quality jobs are offered to handicapped and to long-term unemployed people, which explains the ambivalent reputation of these projects. A similar 'stigma effect' is sometimes observed in recruitment incentive schemes, where the wage cost subsidy 'legitimates' the lower expected productivity of specific target groups; and in mandatory training schemes.

In some countries, local municipalities in charge of social assistance tend to employ their clients just as long as is necessary to transfer them to the (nationally funded) unemployment insurance, without offering genuine reinsertion perspectives. Other carousels are found in programmes where participants can stay for many years without progression or transition to the regular labour market.

Substitution, displacement, dead-weight and competition between target groups (chapter 7)

This means that some measures can have no net job creation effect at all if the new job openings would have existed without the measures (dead-weight). They may perhaps improve the (re)employment probabilities for one group, but at the expense of employment probabilities for other groups of job-seekers (substitution). They may even destroy existing jobs in other firms (displacement). The worst cases of substitution is where some target groups are more privileged in employment programmes than the more disadvantaged groups, thus cutting off the route back to employment for the latter.

As can be seen, the problematic aspects all have a very different nature: political, social, psychological, economic, ... In order to analyse them a multi-disciplinary approach has been adopted, demonstrated by the composition of our network.

Notes

1 Individuals can occupy three positions vis-à-vis the labour market: employed, unemployed or inactive (out of the labour market). Passive labour market measures (career interruption, early retirement, lengthening of compulsory education, ...) aim to transfer individuals from employment or unemployment into inactivity; whereas active measures (training, wage subsidies, ...) aim to transfer unemployed people back to employment.

2 In fact 'active labour market policies' are more ambivalent than our discussion suggests, some measures even aiming to stimulate demand through cost reductions. However, we have deliberately simplified the argument in order to clarify the argument. The parallel existence of demand-stimulating measures does not fundamentally alter our critique anyhow.

3 Barriers to entry

3.1 Introduction

This chapter of the report will examine a number of examples of the way in which the *administrative rules and procedures* applied to active manpower programmes can limit their accessibility to those who need them most.

It is acknowledged that active manpower policies may not be designed explicitly to attack poverty as their primary objective; nevertheless it does seem justifiable to examine their operation in order to question the extent to which they alleviate poverty and social exclusion. The justification for this approach lies in the central role played by the labour market in allocating income to households, and thus the crucial potential of active manpower policies in alleviating poverty by increasing access to the labour market by the poor (Room, 1992; Gaffikin and Morrissey, 1992).

There are a number of ways in which the administrative rules and procedures attached to labour market programmes might act against their full potential in alleviating poverty.

1. *Definition of the boundaries of the labour market*
   This is a consequence of the way in which labour market programmes are often closely linked to the social benefit system. Some population groups are not eligible to claim unemployment insurance or unemployment benefit, and for this reason they are not eligible for labour market programmes. In such a case, administrative eligibility for claiming unemployment benefit also confers eligibility to

gain access to a labour market programme and thus an enhanced opportunity to leave poverty.

2. *Exclusion of marginal workers from mainstream programmes*
This refers to another consequence of the way in which many labour market programmes are closely linked with the social benefit system. Individuals with some form of marginal employment, however inadequate in terms of employment conditions or income, may not be eligible for labour market programmes even though they may be in receipt of some form of income support.

3. *Other eligibility criteria*
Most labour market programmes have a number of eligibility criteria; these are likely to be imposed with reference to the ease of administration, cost considerations, to ideas about their likely effect on the interests of the agency administering the programme, to short-term effects on the national economy, or to political or ideological pressure. In particular, their anticipated value in reducing the official unemployment statistics may be referred to. Their possible beneficial effect on the alleviation of poverty is rarely high on the list of priorities.

3.2 Definition of the boundaries of the labour market

In principle an individual may occupy one of three positions in relation to the labour market; they may be in employment, be unemployed (these two categories together comprising the economically active) or be economically inactive. In reality things are not so clear, as has been demonstrated in chapter 1; but the administration of labour market programmes and demand management concerns related to the resources involved seems to require the creation of rules which rigidly distinguish the economically active from the economically inactive, and within the active group, those who will benefit from programmes and those who will be excluded. This section of the report will be concerned with those rules which reserve labour market programmes for those defined as being properly 'unemployed', and thus disqualifies those defined as being 'out of the labour market' or those with an unclear or ambiguous relationship with the labour market.

3.2.1 Defining the economically active

As the Labour Force Survey clearly illustrates, in some European countries the official register of unemployment does not encompass all those who are seeking work. To take the situation in the UK as an example, the official unemployment statistics are quite explicitly a count of the number of individuals who are claiming unemployment benefit or income support because they are unemployed. This official unemployment count has been subject to academic and political criticism because it excludes numbers of people who would, under other definitions, be included, in order (it is argued) to avoid inflating the unemployment rate.

The differences between the official count and the Labour Force Survey, which uses the International Labour Organisation definition of unemployment, are substantial. One estimate for the UK (based on Lawlor and Kennedy, 1992) is that the number of people looking for work but who were not registered on the official unemployment count, over the years 1984 to 1991 averaged 841,000. In Belgium, 75,000 unemployed aged over 50 are deleted from the unemployment count though still receiving benefits, as are 25,000 who are described as 'exempt from control for family or social reasons'. Similarly, in France, those unemployed who are aged 55 and 3 months are able to receive an allowance (garantie de ressources), but they are considered not to be seeking unemployment any longer.

Single parents in the UK, the 'disabled' in the Netherlands and the older unemployed in Belgium are examples of disadvantaged groups that are considered as being 'out' of the labour market in some countries (yet not in other countries) and therefore ineligible (or eligible only as an exception to the norm) for programmes designed to combat exclusion from employment. Analyses of the living conditions and socio-economic profiles of these groups indicate that many individuals from these groups live in absolute and relative poverty.

In Belgium, the study of the labour market position of the poor reported in chapter 1 showed that 62% of the active poor were fully unemployed, and 15.8% were partly unemployed. Of those who were fully unemployed, about half had unemployment benefits, the other half drawing sickness or disability pensions, the MIG or nothing at all. It must be acknowledged that handicapped people and MIG-receivers have access to specific programmes, but these are generally of limited scope and do by no means compensate for the lack of opportunities to enter mainstream programmes.

Luxembourg has the lowest rate of unemployment in the Community, but it is rising now and might be considered more of a problem in the future. Access to nearly all public training and active manpower programmes for the unemployed is limited to the registered unemployed. The non-registered unemployed group numbers about 50% of the registered, with younger people and women being over-represented; this group, which has no access to active manpower policies, also includes migrant and border workers returning to their country upon losing their job, illegal immigrants and those unemployed people who are withdrawn from the official register because they are within community service programmes.

3.2.2 Excluding sectors of the unemployed

Formal eligibility for reinsertion programmes often requires more than being officially registered as unemployed. The position of people receiving *unemployment insurance* or *minimum income guarantee* (MIG) by virtue of their position in the labour market is a critical issue in this context. In Denmark, for example, there is a particularly clear division between the unemployment insurance system and the social assistance system, where the eligibility conditions for participation in most programmes are determined by two legal statutes. One Act (on Active employment policy) requires that entry should be for unemployed people who are insured (against unemployment) and are eligible for benefits. To become a member of an insurance fund, a person has to be employed, have been employed for a particular qualifying period within the last three years, or be qualified in the subject-area covered by the insurance fund. These conditions are difficult to fulfil for unemployed or unskilled workers. Thus the conditions of access to the unemployment insurance system not only affect the income security of the unemployed, but also their access to reinsertion programmes.

The Danish unemployed who are ineligible for the unemployment insurance system have to apply for help from the social assistance system. Unsurprisingly these MIG-receivers are not really motivated to register as unemployed, as they cannot draw any advantage from it. Only 2/3 of the Danish MIG-receivers are thought to register as unemployed. A second Act (on Activation measures by municipalities) covers people who are unemployed and uninsured, but who receive social assistance (MIG). This enables people under 25 years old to participate in activation schemes only if they receive MIG by virtue of being unemployed; but those over 25 are entitled to participate in activation schemes whatever the reason for their receiving MIG.

In Belgium in 1993, only 475,000 individuals who were 'remunerated full-time unemployed actively seeking work' (ARFU) had access to programmes such as Guidance Plan, Youth Recruitment Plan, or the Enterprise Allowance Scheme. 312,000 other registered unemployed people (including the part-time unemployed, the disabled, MIG-recipients, other unemployed not entitled to benefits, and those older unemployed exempted from control) therefore had no access to the programmes - quite apart from several tens of thousands of *unregistered* unemployed.[1] Although for groups such as the older unemployed it would not be accurate to describe this process as formal exclusion because they have the choice to remain registered as job seekers, the advantages of exemption from control and of higher unemployment benefits appear to be more attractive to the beneficiaries than access to the mediation and guidance services they can expect with reintegration. Similar processes attracted hundreds of thousands to the disability insurance system (WAO) in the Netherlands, until it became obvious that this was causing an almost unbearable burden on social security budgets.

In some countries MIG-receivers are recognised or even privileged as job seekers in legislative initiatives, while they remain excluded de facto. This is the case for those under 25 in Denmark. In Belgium they are officially assimilated to ARFU in some programmes (sometimes they are even subject to positive discrimination in that the required duration of unemployment for entering a scheme is shorter for MIG-receivers than for ARFU). Moreover, since willingness to work is a condition for receiving MIG, most MIG-receivers are forced to register as unemployed when they first apply for the minimum income. Yet in practice less than 20% of the MIG-receivers are found in the unemployment registers (Capet and Kervyn, 1991). It is reported that their registrations are deleted every three months so that they do not inflate the unemployment statistics unnecessarily,[2] a practice noted in France also. An unintended side-effect of this practice, however, is that they do not receive any job or training offer once they have disappeared from the registers. Among the Flemish unemployed (using a broad definition), MIG-receivers represent 8% of the population while their share in direct employment programmes and training is estimated to be less than 1% (Nicaise, 1993).

Still other countries exclude some groups from the minimum income guarantee (MIG), and therefore unintentionally from those pro-

---

grammes which are linked to receipt of the minimum income guarantee. This is the case in France, where large families are often excluded from receiving the MIG because their family allowance is higher than the threshold of MIG, and for those single parents (who are mostly women) with children below the age of three receiving the single parent allowance (API = allocation de parent isolé). Their income is higher than it would if they received MIG, but they lose access to the reinsertion measures linked to receipt of the MIG. This becomes a problem for them, especially single parents, when their circumstances change or their children get older and their allowances decrease to the lower level of MIG. By that time they have often lost contact with the labour market.

In Luxembourg, some groups are ineligible for MIG; those who are under 30 years old (except for single parents, the second of a couple of parents, the disabled and carers), those not legally resident in Luxembourg, and those who have stayed (legally) in Luxembourg for less than 10 years. In practice some young people may gain access to an income in the form of a participation allowance by becoming registered with employment agencies, but these exceptions make it no easier for the young who live by themselves or with their parents to gain access to schemes, nor for the homeless.

3.3 Exclusion of marginal workers from mainstream programmes

Individuals who are able to get employment, but employment which is inadequate because it is marginal, are unable to take advantage of most labour market programmes because of their eligibility criteria. This section of the chapter is therefore concerned with those people working in the marginal sectors of the labour market including many who are effectively trapped in this sector and who are in poverty; it is important to distinguish this group from those who may be working in these sectors of the labour market but who are not in poverty, perhaps students or people who do occasional work to contribute to a family income which is, overall, relatively high.

An agreed transnational definition of what constitutes the 'marginal' labour market does not exist. This term might encompass the following forms of employment:
- temporary employment;
- seasonal employment;
- homeworkers (that is people who work for an employer but who carry out the work in their own homes, typically women who do low-

skilled and low-waged work, although some people who are highly skilled and well-paid work in their own homes);
- part-time workers;
- sheltered employment;
- work-experience participants;
- those on 'absorption' programmes.

The two most important categories from the perspective of this report are probably:
- those who unwillingly experience frequent periods of unemployment between temporary jobs, and;
- those who work part-time because they are unable to gain full-time employment.

Examples of how the eligibility rules for labour market programmes tend to exclude these groups are common as they are generally targeted at those who are unemployed (that is, not those in part-time work), and have been unemployed for a long period (which would exclude many of those whose employment pattern involves periods of interspersed employment and unemployment).

In the UK eligibility for labour market programmes is closely linked to the *period of time* a person has been registered as a claimant for unemployment benefit; different programmes become accessible after different periods of unemployment. The official explanation for this is that it is most economically efficient to target resources on those people who are most in need (that is, those people who have not been able to get back into work fairly quickly). Each episode of unemployment begins a new time period, so a person who repeatedly leaves the unemployment register, perhaps to undertake short spells of seasonal work, will never reach the important six-month threshold which provides access to a Training for Work scheme which could provide a qualification and thus a more stable employment pattern. (Periods of very short-term work, up to 28 days, are excluded from this rule).

In Belgium, the Fourth World Movement has noted the complaints of people who point out that different definitions of what constitutes 'long-term unemployment' can apply to different issues, to the disadvantage of those people who do get occasional work but wish to take advantage of a programme. Thus, while intermittent employment is considered as not breaking a period of unemployment when a reduction of benefit (for becoming LTU) is at stake, it does constitute a break

in a period of unemployment (for becoming LTU) which is a require-
ment of entering a programme.

As concerns *part-time workers*, information provided by Eurostat,
based upon the Labour Force Survey, illustrates how part-time work is
expanding across Europe as a whole, and considerably in some countries. Between 1983 and 1991, the percentage of workers in part-time
employment increased by around 11% in the Netherlands, and more
than 3% in Belgium and the UK. Across Europe as a whole, the increase
was around 3%; only in Denmark and Greece was there a decrease in
the proportion of the employed labour force which was in part-time
work. Yet most labour market programmes exclude this increasing
group of workers, many of whom occupy precarious jobs.

3.4 Other eligibility criteria - the reverse side of positive discrimination

The two previous sections deal with the most common eligibility criteria of labour market programmes; these are the need to be registered as
unemployed (in ways which vary between countries), to be insured or
remunerated, and to have remained continuously in that state for a
specified period of time, usually six or twelve months. There are also a
number of less theoretical conditions (for example, age limits or, or the
need to be a woman returning to the labour market) which apply to
every programme. By their very nature, eligibility conditions are an
exclusion mechanism, yet alongside these there are examples of programmes which involve mandatory attendance or compulsion. It is
however beyond the scope of this study to examine these numerous
conditions in detail.

There are many examples of exceptions to the normal eligibility criteria for many programmes, which results in a form of positive discrimination; for example in the UK exceptions may be made for
women who are returning to economic activity after child-rearing, for
recently released prisoners, for people with disabilities, for people recently quitting the armed forces, for those with difficulty with literacy
or numeracy, and in other special cases such as in localities with large-
scale redundancies.

In Belgium MIG-receivers with the status of 'head of household', and
those under 25 years of age enjoy priority treatment in some cases,
while in France there is a general category for exemption for those ex-
periencing problems with exclusion, as well as priority status for those
unemployed for longer than three years, for MIG-recipients who have

---

been unemployed for more than one year, for unemployed people of over 50 and for people with disabilities.

The problems encountered by older workers and unemployed people in France have been especially recognised by giving them priority status for certain measures (at 50 plus), and by introducing pre-retirement measures aimed specifically at older (55 or over) people.

In Luxembourg the criteria for entry to courses are expressed in terms of priorities for particular groups rather than the exclusion or inclusion of particular groups. It has been argued that this leads to a kind of creaming-off, with the least attractive candidates (MIG recipients) being offered only the least popular courses. This criticism has been recognised in Luxembourg, with non-governmental organisations (NGO's) developing courses for those who may be unable or unwilling to go on to publicly-provided courses, and with public courses also being developed for MIG recipients. There are also courses specifically for women returners (no male candidates accepted despite many applications) and for the disabled unemployed. However, this example serves to illustrate that well constructed and appropriate eligibility criteria are probably necessary to enable disadvantaged groups to benefit from programmes and that an 'open-door' policy may well result in less, not more, opportunity for the disadvantaged.

While there are clearly examples of good practice aimed at positive discrimination, one question which must be asked is how far these priorities are substantiated by objective studies of the relative disadvantage of different groups. Another question is how well the rules are publicised to the population groups who would benefit most by taking advantage of them. It must also be acknowledged that priority rules tend to make legislation and administration more complex - sometimes even incoherent - and that in some cases they are rather designed for reasons of demand management than for social reasons. In any case, the coexistence of well-intended positive discrimination in favour of the poor with barriers to entry in general is a paradox that calls for particular attention in future policy.

3.5 Conclusions and policy implications

The experience of national policies reviewed in this chapter shows, once again, that the term 'exclusion from the labour market' is not value-free. It reveals how the marginal position of some groups vis-à-vis the labour market is more or less consciously reinforced by barriers that prevent them from participation in reinsertion programmes.

Some of the mechanisms are related to the very foundations of our social protection systems: the meritocratic rules of access to continental social security systems are implicitly transposed into the reintegration programmes, which in turn - despite attempts to target on more disadvantaged groups - are tailored to the needs of the median (unemployed) worker: the full-time, registered, healthy, insured unemployed (thus, the previously full-time, stable, healthy worker).

Other mechanisms betray the inability of bureaucracies to cope effectively with the needs of the poorest: when trying to reach the most disadvantaged, they establish complex and sometimes incoherent eligibility rules that fail to take into account the diversity of situations of disadvantage, thereby excluding other candidates who are equally worthy of consideration, and reducing the attractiveness of incentives to employers.

However, this chapter has not only shown failures, but also examples of good practice and lessons that can be drawn from past experiences. In what follows, we try to sum up briefly the main recommendations that can be derived from the analysis. They will be recapitulated more extensively in the final chapter of the report.

1. If active manpower programmes are to have a role in combating poverty, then it should be possible for any individual to register their interest in benefiting from such programmes as exist in each member state. The simple way for this to be achieved is to make it a right of any job-seeker (whether remunerated/receiving benefit or not) to register their interest in gaining access to active manpower programmes and the advice and guidance which is available from Employment Services/Agencies. For some categories relying on other sectors of social security (e.g. MIG-receivers, disabled persons, single parents) automatic registration could even facilitate the registration procedure.

2. Employment Services/Agencies should, where they do not now do so, treat all job-seekers on an equal basis; the only qualification for gaining assistance from the Government Agency should be honest the desire to gain employment, or to gain more suitable employment. An exception to this would be where positive discrimination for particularly disadvantaged groups is the norm. Quotas to ensure that weaker groups are being included might usefully be set where these exceptions are established.

3. Where exceptions are currently made to eligibility criteria in order to positively discriminate in favour of groups who are thought to be disadvantaged, this should be widely publicised. The priority rules should not be established on an ad hoc basis; they should rather be based on objective in-depth studies of the relative disadvantage of different groups, e.g. their relative outflow probabilities from unemployment. Complex priority rules should be avoided.

4. Specific eligibility or priority criteria based upon the length of unemployment serve a useful purpose where they are applied sensitively in order to target scarce resources upon those most in need. It is however questionable whether the length of the last unbroken spell of unemployment applied rigidly is a very good discriminator of need.

Notes

[1] Among them, 80% of the MIG-recipients = 46,000.

[2] From an administrative point of view, it is difficult to establish when a MIG-receiver has found a job, if he/she does not inform the employment agency about it spontaneously. For insured unemployed, this is easier as the agency is automatically informed as soon as the entitlement to benefits has expired. The automatic deletion of MIG-receivers is thus used to avoid them remaining registered too long after having found a job.

4 Mismatches between provisions and needs

4.1 Introduction

After having examined the problem of accessibility of labour market programmes in chapter 3, the present chapter deals more with their content and process. It addresses the question of whether the provisions correspond to the needs of the unemployed as well as the needs of industry (i.e. the needs of the labour market). To be efficient, any labour market provision must, one way or another, take both considerations into account.

The analysis in this chapter will be mainly focused on training provisions, but many of the conclusions can be transferred to other types of labour market provision.

4.2 Mismatches between provisions and the needs of the unemployed

Labour market provisions that are combating long-term unemployment should take account of differences between the needs and aspirations of various disadvantaged groups. Experience shows that, in order to achieve good results, provisions should be based on the needs of the unemployed in at least three ways. Firstly, the provisions should correspond to the capabilities and knowledge level of the unemployed to whom they apply. Secondly, they should reflect some kind of (more or less) conscious wish on the part the unemployed. These rules apply, mutatis mutandis, to the programmes and provisions aimed at including the more disadvantaged job-seekers. In a context of poverty, moreover, a third condition is that psychological and material constraints be removed in order to allow people to take risks and invest in their own future.

Studies on the training/employment needs and aspirations of the unemployed in general, and of the most vulnerable groups in particular, are surprisingly scarce. Hence, a first recommendation to policy makers could be to stimulate this kind of studies, with a strong involvement of the field workers who are active in this area as well as the (potential) participants.

4.2.1 Meeting the capabilities of disadvantaged groups

High and persistent unemployment can result in a polarisation in the labour market, where the disadvantaged groups are in high risk of exclusion from the labour market, as is the case in Denmark (Pedersen, 1994). In this case even an economic growth will not change the position of these groups in the labour market, but will result in a greater mobility for the stronger groups. In order to improve the employability of the disadvantaged groups it is often necessary to upgrade or change their skills through (pre)vocational training.

However, training courses will not be effective if they fail to recognise the capabilities, the level of existing knowledge and the confidence level of the unemployed to whom they apply. If the level is too low, the result may be demotivation and perhaps subsequently dropout. This was one of the major problems with the implementation of the Danish training courses for the long-term unemployed (Christiansen, 1990). If the level is too high, the provision is simply a waste of resources.

To enhance the qualifications of disadvantaged groups requires that training is considered as one element of an integration programme and should be tailored to the need of individuals. Often, disadvantaged groups need *long training trajectories combined with on-the-job training and general social assistance*. However, labour market provisions used by the weaker groups of unemployed are paradoxically often of shorter duration and less individualised than the provisions used by the stronger groups. In Denmark this applies for the training courses and job offers in the public sector (Thaulow and Anker, 1991). An evaluation study for ESF-objectives 3-4 in Belgium (Nicaise e.a., 1994 - forthcoming) indicates that:
- courses offered to long-term unemployed (objective 3) have on average a shorter duration than those offered to youngsters (objective 4);

- the duration of courses offered to disadvantaged groups by NGO Programmes and the public sector varies. Public courses which are segmented into a pre-training stage and qualifying courses do not go much further than the first stage. NGO courses which are small in quantity seem to be able to integrate both phases.

Experience from Luxembourg supports the hypothesis that NGO-programmes are more than public programmes based on the needs and capabilities of disadvantaged groups. Public training programmes are generally too exclusively specialised and content oriented, making it difficult for the weaker groups to use them. For instance, courses offered by a large public training centre can be classified in the following:
- 72% of the training courses give priority to candidates who are working in that specific branch (or preparing some specific certificate) or to candidates who have previous experience within that branch and are registered as unemployed;
- 21% require no former experience in the subject area, but registration as unemployed is a prerequisite to attend courses;
- barely 7% have free access for all unemployed, i.e. (prior) experience or registration as unemployed is not an explicit condition.

Some provisions with relatively good employment effects are seldom used to integrate the more disadvantaged groups. When it does happen, these groups generally achieve far less success than the stronger ones, which again may indicate a mismatch between the schemes in general and the capabilities of the most deprived unemployed. The problem is partly caused by the fact that little importance is attached to the need to adapt the provision to the individual needs of the unemployed, for example by including special options such as introductory courses or follow up activities. This has been the case with vocational training courses in Denmark. According to a panel study that covers the year 1976-1986, vocational training courses have had a positive impact on wages of employed workers (mainly skilled workers) and have reduced their subsequent unemployment. The same courses, however, have had a *negative* employment effect[1] for long-term unemployed participants (Jensen e.a., 1991). Other reasons for this failure are thought to be (a) the poor quality of some courses; (b) the lack of motivation among long-term unemployed people, who were obliged to attend them; and (c) bad timing of the (compulsory) training schemes for the long-term unemployed.

4.2.2 Meeting the motivations of disadvantaged groups

In Denmark, under the previous labour market policy (modified in January 1994), long-term unemployed people were obliged to participate in training courses in order to be entitled to unemployment benefits for another 3 years (under the new policies, they can choose between several measures). Therefore some long-term unemployed participated in training courses solely to re-establish the right to unemployment insurance benefits. This could be one of the reasons for the lower achievement levels of long-term unemployed people after participation in training courses.

What are the motivations of the poor ?

It is sometimes argued that the low-skilled and the long-term unemployed are - paradoxically - less motivated to participate in traditional training schemes than other job-seekers. Is there evidence for this view ? If it is true, what are the real needs of these groups ? Labour market provision needs to try to meet these aspirations. Many studies have shown that far better results are achieved when participants are motivated for what they are doing (Aakrog, 1991).

Many studies indicate that disadvantaged groups prefer to have a job rather than participating in training courses. However, they are willing to take part in training, if it really helps them to find employment.

In Denmark, it seems that some groups are only interested in getting a job and do not look at training as an investment. This is especially the case for unskilled workers and some migrants. If the educational provisions are optional, these groups seldom use them. If they can choose between employment projects or education, they typically choose what is most similar to real work.

In Luxembourg about 15% of MIG beneficiaries are obliged to participate in training or insertion programmes. They can choose between community work and training. The following figures show that preferences are obviously in favour of community work. The evolution of the number of contracts according to type in table 4.1 shows the relative success of community work compared to training.

Table 4.1
Trends in integration contracts with MIG-receivers in Luxembourg, according to type

Year	Training	Community work
1986	6	0
1987	23	140
1988	89	256
1989	55	402
1990	59	412
1991	71	384
1992	91	429

Two other evaluation studies from Luxembourg shed some additional light on the motivation of the unemployed for participating in training programmes. The first one, relating to training programmes for LTU and youngsters cofinanced by the ESF, is summarised in table 4.2.

Table 4.2
Reasons for participation in training programmes cofinanced by the ESF, in %

Get a higher level of qualification	19
Find a job	46
Get a better job	11
Administrative compulsion (entitlement to benefits)	18
Other	6
Total	100

Another study within the PETRA programme (Wagner, 1990) has evaluated public and private initial vocational training programmes for low-skilled youngsters. When asked about their plans after the training period, 92% answered that they would like to get a job. Only 8% of the participants had planned to go on with training.

In the UK, Lynn (1992) quotes 97% of participants on Employment Training wanting work rather than training. They participate in training courses in order to improve their employment chances.

A survey of long-term unemployed, conducted by De Witte (1993)[2] in Belgium, shows a different picture. Among the average long-term unemployed:

- 65% would like to work again within 6 months (16% do not want to work ever again);
- 47% of those willing to work would prefer to work half-time;
- 66% would accept to attend a training course if necessary;
- 68% would accept a temporary (6 months') job;
- less than 50% would accept a monotonous job, or a job at a lower qualification or remuneration level, irregular work hours, etc.

In other words, LTU would not simply accept any kind of work, while on the other hand, they are not really avert from training 'if it is a necessary condition to find work'.

Furthermore, whereas the average long-term unemployed appear to have some commitment to training, there are notable differences between subgroups. Less qualified and older long-term unemployed would rather work and are less willing to retrain or accept precarious jobs. These observations are confirmed by the profile of participants in 'Weer-Werk-Actie' (back to work action which recruits long-term unemployed on a voluntary basis for career guidance, possibly linked with training and work experience). This programme has tended to attract the relatively younger and better qualified among the target group.

De Witte's differentiated picture opens the debate about *typologies* of motivations among the unemployed in general, and the most disadvantaged job-seekers in particular. There is not much literature on this subject. Godinot, who has been leading several reinsertion projects for the ATD-Fourth World, suggests that four types of motivation may be distinguished among participants from poor families:
- the first group shows a preference for work rather than training. Often their preference for a job is due to a mixture of financial motives and repeated disappointments in previous education and training efforts, which make them anxious about new failure risks;
- a second group, consisting of totally unqualified and often illiterate people, prefers to combine work with training, in order to reconcile the need for an immediate income with an unavoidable long-term investment in training;
- a third group, consisting mainly of young women without children, has a marked preference for full-time training courses, provided that they receive adequate remuneration. Given the present high level of unemployment, it would be wise to 'use the opportunity' and to invest heavily in the human capital of such people;

- finally, some individuals are not really aspiring neither to have a job, nor to get training; they are interested to participate in a scheme as far as it includes a remuneration.

A study on AIF (Actions d'insertion et de formation) in France identifies 4 types of trainees with different motivation levels (Chérain et Demazière, 1991 and 1992):
- group 1: who do not regard training as an investment in human capital but as a way of spending their time. They are usually 45-50 years old and feel that they have a handicap of age or health that cannot be altered through training. Their attitude towards their opportunities in finding a job in the future is fatalistic and they are waiting to withdraw from the labour market fully. They have had stable jobs previously and became unemployed due to sluggish economic growth;
- group 2: who prefer to have direct access to work but accept the opportunity of training to improve their employment chances. They have never invested heavily in education or training. They are 37-47 years old and have experienced unemployment periods of shorter duration which have, over time, lengthened;
- group 3: who accept training as a last resort. They have been unemployed for a long time and see their prolonged unemployment as a dead end, and their attempts to overcome it lead to repeated failures. They show negative attitudes towards all the provisions and have no or only loose contact to the labour market. They are 26-42 years old and are at risk of becoming marginalized;
- group 4: who see training as a way of coping with uncertainty related to unemployment. They are 26-36 years old and have experienced only precarious or short term jobs.

Our analysis in this subsection leads us to the conclusion that disadvantaged groups generally prefer work to training, although this preference should not be interpreted as an aversion to training. It is not surprising, after all, that jobless people do not appreciate the intrinsic value of training when their first need is a job. What appears to be more paradoxical is that among the unemployed, those with the longest duration, older age groups, and the least qualified appear to be less keen to enter a training scheme.

In trying to understand this paradox, researchers and practitioners have formulated the following hypotheses:

- risky investment

Especially in the context of training policies, it should be acknowledged that reinsertion implies an 'investment' on the part of the unemployed: not only do they have to bear a number of expenses (transport costs, child care, learning materials, ...), but also, and even more important, they are supposed to postpone job seeking activities and thus to lengthen their expected unemployment duration in the short run. On the other hand, the outcome of the investment is far from certain. If the general experience is that training courses do not reduce the subsequent unemployment substantially, it is quite rational to hesitate to participate. Evaluation of specific provisions for disadvantaged people in Belgium shows that training raises the employment probability 6 months after attending from about 20 to 40% (see table A.4 in appendix). However positive this result may be, it still implies that most trainees do not find a job (Nicaise e.a., 1994 - forthcoming).

- fear of failure

Unemployed who have never been successful at school can be afraid of attending training courses. In this case, especially when there is not much correspondence between the training courses and their capabilities, it can result in repeated failure and high drop out rates or low achievement levels.

- financial thresholds

Job-seekers who have temporary part time jobs or marginal earnings from a few hours work in the informal sector would have to forego some income. The cost of living would increase because of the extra expenses they would have. Even if a training allowance is provided, and if material costs incurred by training are reimbursed, the postponement of additional income through reduced job search in the short run may constitute an unbearable investment on the part of trainees, and might prevent them from (long-term) participation.

- non-correspondence of training to needs and aspirations of long-term unemployed

When training courses are not tailored to the needs of individuals they are not motivated to participate. Sometimes, disadvantaged groups are obliged to take part in the measures or they will be excluded from unemployment system. But, what is the outcome of mandatory provision ? We discuss this in the following subsection.

In general, problems regarding motivation are typically found in compulsory provisions. On the one hand, compulsory schemes are 'egalitarian' in that they imply guarantees of job and/or training offers to all unemployed, including the most disadvantaged. On the other hand, when unemployed people are forced - by virtue of the existing rules - into an activity, it can take a lot of energy and resources to change their attitudes for the better (examples of this can be observed in the context of the Danish youth allowance scheme, where a predominant reason for breaking off the participation is that 'it wasn't interesting enough'). The outcome of the provisions in general seem to be better if they are based on voluntary participation. Examples of this can be observed in the Danish education allowance for self-chosen education (Thaulow and Anker, 1992; Pilegard e.a., 1991).

Where a particular labour market programme is compulsory, it is important that the supply is adequate to meet demand, not just in overall terms but also at times and in places where the demand exists. While a shortfall in provision is obviously a problem, it is the consequences of a breakdown in provision of this type which is important. The consequences could simply mean a longer wait if the rules are interpreted sympathetically; but they might be severe for those individuals who are unable to get on to a form of provision if this is a condition of receiving some form of income support, or if a form of competition between applicants results.

In Denmark, for example, the demand for vocational training (AMU-training) exceeds the extent of available provision. This has resulted in a form of competition in which the most disadvantaged jobseekers find it very difficult to get an offer of a training place while the less disadvantaged do much better. It has been even more difficult for the non-insured long-term unemployed to find a training place. The compulsory nature of the provision means that they will be referred to courses they are not interested in. The system thus exacerbates to some extent the consequences of labour market disadvantage rather than eradicating it.

It is often the scheme of 'job-offer' (now called job training) that gives the unemployed access to these training courses. Thus even though many unemployed wish to participate in training courses, they are not able to do so before they are long-term unemployed. By that time, it appears that the effect of training can not outweigh the stigma of long-term unemployment itself.

The new Danish Labour Market policy (put into effect in January 1994) attempts to solve this problem. Relating to disadvantaged groups, the main improvements are decentralisation of the provision, and offering help at an early stage of unemployment. Under the new rules, the unemployed do not need to wait 2 years to receive a job offer. They have a right to draw up their own action plan (time table) and choose to have a job-training period at an early stage of their unemployment. The aim is to match the individual needs with those of the local labour market. Much emphasis is put on guidance and orientation of the unemployed before making an action-plan. Another principle is that unemployed people with a knowledge of the labour market and employment chances combine on-the-job training (subsidised jobs in the private or the public sectors) with education or (pre)vocational training. The result of an evaluation study of the 'action plan' scheme in one pilot-region (Ribe Amt) indicates that most participants (82%) are satisfied with the scheme,[3] although variables such as age and education are important influences on the level of their satisfaction (Linde, 1994). However, these provisions are so new that it is not possible to fully evaluate the way in which these regulations will work, nor whether they will solve some of the existing problems (such as shortage of AMU-training).

In the UK, it has been argued that changes in legislation which were designed to ensure that young people (aged 16 to 18) are either in education, in employment or in vocational training have resulted in numbers of young people becoming homeless or otherwise marginalized. This is because income support was withdrawn from those aged 16-18 unless they were registered as attending a Youth Training (YT) scheme (those in employment receive wages and those in education are assumed to be supported by families). Since there was a shortfall in provision of YT places this left a number of young people with no income. The number of places for YT has fallen from 389,224 in march 1988 to 274,000 in 1993. It is estimated that around 50,000 homeless are living in London alone and about 150,000 youngsters become homeless each year (The Guardian, June 1st, 1994). There has been an attempt to ameliorate this situation recently by changes in the rules on income support payments, but the basic situation remains unchanged.

Similar drawbacks have been noted in the Netherlands with the introduction of the Youth Guarantee Act (JWG = Jeugdwerkgarantiewet) in 1992. The objective of this law is to guarantee a temporary job to every person below the age of 20 who has been unemployed for more than one year; the law will be gradually extended to all young long-term unemployed people below the age of 26. At this early stage of implementation, the scheme covers just over half of the target group; it is known that some of the most disadvantaged have not yet been reached (migrant girls, totally unskilled youngsters not covered by social protection, youngsters from families living in caravans or boats, ...). Moreover, as the supply (of youngsters) exceeds the demand (on the part of employers), and as the JWG-jobs are 100% subsidised, some employers have concluded so-called 'empty contracts' without really engaging the youngsters at their workplace. As a consequence of this improper use of the scheme, 8,000 youngsters have lost their entitlement to unemployment benefits (de Koning, 1994).

It would be a mistake, however, to conclude that these types of programmes have no merit at all. The remarks on the perverse effects of guarantee schemes and mandatory schemes should be weighted against the positive aspects of these schemes in terms of the redistribution of opportunities, the reduction of long-term unemployment, increased transition into regular employment, etc. It must be possible to avoid the negative side-effects, for example, by increasing the number of (high-quality) places available, by offering a wide range of options, and by disconnecting the individual's entitlement to work from his/her entitlement to social security - or at least, by providing for a proper equilibrium between rights and duties.

4.2.3 Psychological and material constraints

There is considerable evidence that (long-term) unemployment is associated with distress which affects psychological health. There is a great variation in the degree of experienced stress and the methods unemployed people use to deal with it. In this respect social and economic resources available to the unemployed, and their coping skills are among the important factors. It is widely accepted that psychological well-being affects the intensity of job search, and the motivation level of the unemployed to participate in programmes (James, 1993).

One of the distressing factors related to unemployment is financial strain: for many it is the lack of money which is the worst thing about unemployment. As stated earlier, the unemployed have to bear the expenses for participation in labour market measures, which adds to the financial strain. When reinsertion programmes fail to take these psychological and financial constraints into account, it is not surprising that dropout rates are higher and outcomes poorer than expected.

The lack of adequate remuneration, as a means to help overcoming elementary material problems, results in non participation of some unemployed people in labour market programmes. A problem noted in the UK is that attendance on a labour market programme can create difficulties because it demands attendance and behaviour similar to that experienced in employment, but it does not offer the degree of remuneration that would compensate an employee for long hours of attendance. One particular difficulty is faced by unemployed women with child care responsibilities; whilst unemployed they do not require child care assistance, and if employed they could afford to pay for it. But the degree of remuneration on a labour market programme (typically £10 a week more than their benefit level) does not provide sufficient funds to allow them to purchase child care assistance to attend the programme. This problem has been recognised and allowances are now sometimes payable to remedy this problem.

In France, trainees have had to give up training courses, especially in rural areas, because of similar material obstacles, like child care, access to transport or accommodation when the training location is remote from home. Some trainers and social workers have realised that material constraints prevent disadvantaged groups from participating in programmes. Thus, often at the initiative of local authorities, specific actions are in place to remedy this. In Thionville (Lorraine), in deprived neighbourhoods, mothers can buy lunch for their children at very low prices, so that they do not have to spend time making lunch and can undergo training. In Metz (Lorraine), unemployed people get some access to child care facilities. In Rennes (Bretagne), Beneficiaries of MIG have a right to a travel card on all public transport.

The problem of adequate remuneration is not a simple one, however: in some cases it can itself become an obstacle in the transition towards the regular labour market, when the income difference between trainees and employed workers is low, or even negative when account is taken of in-kind services to trainees. Examples of such 'barriers to exit' have been noted in Denmark, for example. This is examined in chapter 6.

4.3 Mismatches between provisions and the needs of the labour market

If the objective of labour market programmes is to integrate the participants into the labour market, it seems important that they are not only adapted to the needs of the unemployed, but also to the needs of the labour market. Broadly speaking, this means that the qualifications which the provisions are intended to impart to the participants should correspond to the qualifications needed in the labour market, in the short or the long term.

Unfortunately, there are great difficulties in establishing the needs of the labour market. It is a very abstract concept, which is very difficult to transform into concrete educational requirements. The present recession makes it even more difficult. This problem is evident from several Danish attempts at describing these needs (Pilegaard e.a., 1991; Aarkrog e.a., 1991; Maerkedahl e.a., 1992).

At present, there is no method of measuring the needs of the labour market directly. Indirectly, however, different approaches can be used as indications of how the labour market reacts to the qualifications acquired. Post-training employment rates seem to be the most straightforward parameters. If they live up to the demands of the labour market, the participants should do well in the competition for vacant jobs and have a high employment rate. If they do not live up to the demands, they will have a low employment rate. In Denmark it is well documented that the weaker groups have employment rates far below the stronger groups. This applies to rehabilitation benefits (AKF, 1986), job offers (both private and public sector), education allowances for self-chosen education, training courses (Thaulow and Anker, 1992) and youth allowances (Engelund e.a., 1992).

However, employment rates at some fixed point after the training has been completed are influenced by so many different (demand and supply) factors that they can not be considered very useful indicators of the match between provisions and needs of the labour market. This holds a fortiori for differential employment rates according to the group characteristics of the participants, as it is impossible to isolate the influence of the provisions from other influences.

A somewhat more sophisticated approach consists in surveys where previous trainees who have found a job are asked to what extent their later occupation(s) correspond to the content of the training they have received. This approach has been used for Belgium in several regional evaluation studies in the past (Lux, 1984 for Mons; Simoens, 1993 for the 'Kempen'). Lux and Simoens both find 'non-correspondence' ratios of about 1/3. A similar type of analysis is included in the current Belgian evaluation of programmes co-financed by the ESF (Nicaise e.a., 1995) which distinguishes between provisions for disadvantaged groups and other provisions. As can be expected, prevocational training programmes, which are most relevant for disadvantaged groups, have a lower correspondence ratio between job and training than vocational training (see table A.4 in the appendix). But here again, the results may be biased, this time for another reason. It must be noted that concurrence between training and job is measured on the basis of a subjective evaluation of trainees. In prevocational training, the general skills and social attitudes make a relatively large part of the courses. Trainees might not have accounted for these elements when they judged the utility of the training for the specific job they have found. Thus correspondence rate between training and job is probably underestimated for prevocational training.

Nevertheless, from table A.4 (in the appendix) it appears that even in the case of more advanced vocational training (e.g. VDAB-secondary and tertiary sector training courses)[4] there is 30 to 40% non-concurrence between training and job, while VDAB individual training in enterprise has the highest correspondence ratio.

A third indirect way to evaluate the correspondence between training programmes and the needs of the labour market is in regression analysis with cross-section and time series data on the composition of the training supply on the one hand, and of vacancies on the other (see Lux, 1984). This approach has the disadvantage that it does not use micro-data, and hence, does not allow for differentiation between disadvantaged and other groups.

Notwithstanding the difficulties encountered in measuring the phenomenon of (mis)matching, there is much 'anecdotal' evidence of provisions for disadvantaged groups being geared towards weak labour market segments. This applies to training as well as job creation projects, especially in small-scale, local initiatives.

The economic potential for local initiatives of this sort is small. Attempts to develop businesses and create jobs through initiatives in the 'classic' economic sector often run aground because of competition and the resistance of companies active in the sector in question. On the other hand, new economic sectors (high-tech industries, information technology, electronics and communications) are still underdeveloped in Europe and they are often beyond the reach of local initiatives (because of a lack of expertise, professionalism and funding on the part of the instigators of the schemes, plus the inadequate qualifications of those taking part in the initiatives). Thus, local initiatives tend to work well in areas that are not brand new but have been abandoned by companies for failing to give an adequate return on investment. Several studies of local projects in Europe show that a good number of them tend to offer training or employment in traditional activities such as recycling, clearing and renovation, gardening, restoration, neighbourhood services, promoting local products, or activities carried out in the context of farm co-operatives.

Within the framework of 'Contrats emploi solidarité' (CES) in France, participants are offered activities like gardening or maintenance jobs without any thought for more gratifying activities and without any incentives to participate in a qualification programme.

The choice of offered activities may also have an impact on the financial situation of the projects - as illustrated in the evaluation study of 'social workshops' in Flanders (Vanhuysse and Henkes, 1992): poor outcomes (in financial terms) in some local projects are not solely attributed to the personal characteristics of the target group but also to an inappropriate choice of proposed activities (gardening, maintenance, recycling activities, subcontracting, ...) whereas activities within the industrial sector bring better results.

Inappropriate funding methods may themselves affect the labour market outcomes of provisions. A study of ET (Employment Training - now 'Training for work') in the UK by Alan Felstead (1994) indicates that this programme is largely inclined to provide skills which are not in much demand. A network of legally independent local companies (TECs = Training-Enterprise Councils/LECs = Local Enterprise Councils), funded by the government, are charged to provide training and enterprise programmes. The government try to enhance value for money through the funding system of the operation of TECs/LECs. Paradoxically, however, the funding system does not stimulate TECs/LECs to take much account of the occupational area or the type of trainees. When the cost per output in some area such as construction and engineering trades is higher, the TECs/LECs have more economic incentives to provide output in low-cost area such as clerical and secretarial occupations. This will result firstly in excess supply of these areas. A second consequence is that training providers are being segmented into providers of specialists (Colleges of further Education or dedicated workshops) and large providers of low skill trainees. Thirdly, the provider of training may choose those who are most likely to achieve good results and discriminate against those who need most help.

Another type of mismatch relates to the lack of progression within training provision. As a response to the needs of its target groups, some providers tend to specialise in supplying basic training (initial training or pre-vocational training), even though it is not always possible to include this type of training in a more complete curriculum. As a result, it is not always possible to switch from pre-vocational to vocational training proper and there may be a conflict between the starting level and the rules for gaining access to vocational training.

Qualifications that are not recognised or for which there is no demand, inaccessible qualifications, and a lack of comprehensive training itineraries - all of these things are sources of frustration for the participants, because in the final analysis it is their chances of finding work again that are being affected.

It is important that training of disadvantaged groups is considered to be a process, a trajectory by which the needs of the labour market are matched stepwise with the needs of job-seekers. Relatively good results can be achieved when prevocational courses are integrated with vocational courses and are combined with 'on the job training'. There are examples of successful training programmes that have tried to meet these needs.

One example of good practice is 'alternating education' in Belgium which was launched in Flanders on an experimental basis in 1985. Alternating education is a combination of general and vocational instruction at school with complementary training and work experience in firms. It involves a strong (organisational and financial) partnership between schools and social partners. This programme was especially designed to meet the needs of disadvantaged and school-fatigued youngsters in the context of the lengthening of compulsory education until the age of 18. By combining part-time education and part time work, the transition of school-fatigued youngsters who where strongly work-oriented was eased. An evaluation study of this programme reveals that the programme has a high qualitative employment effect, i.e. (relative to other part time education) there is a better correspondence between training and job, jobs are more stable and consequently better terms of contract are achieved (Nicaise and Douterlungne, 1991). Another follow up study of the 1988 cohort of participants in alternating education reports a 100% employment rate after 4 years, compared to a significantly lower rate of the comparison group (Nijsmans and Nicaise, 1994).

In Denmark, the new labour market reform tries to give more flexibility for adjustment of labour market measures according to the need of the local labour market. Flexibility of the measures makes it possible to take better account of the needs of individuals and the labour market. It is the local labour market authorities who, on the basis of local conditions and needs, decide on matters like the targets for the initiatives in the regions, the type of initiatives, and priorities that should be given to initiatives, including identification of target groups.

4.4 Conclusions and policy implications

It is widely believed that one of the main supply-side factors hindering integration of disadvantaged groups into the labour market is their lack or low level of *general and vocational education*. Often reselling or upgrading of disadvantaged groups is seen as a precondition for their placement in the labour market. Therefore participation in training courses and/or other provisions is made compulsory in some countries. From an egalitarian point of view compulsory provisions may be useful if at the same time they guarantee access to provision by all the unemployed, including the most disadvantaged. It is, however, generally acknowledged that, when trainees are free to study their preferred subject, they will be more motivated to learn and improve their qualifications. Guarantees can also be given without compulsion.

As far as decision makers feel that compulsion should be maintained, a sufficient supply of provision appears to be an essential condition. Experience has shown that insufficient provision in so-called guarantee systems has led to new forms of inequality and exclusion.

Mismatches between provisions and the *needs of the unemployed,* can result in demotivation and low achievement of participants. Some of the long-term unemployed have had problems at school and their fear of the repeated failure can prevent them from attending courses. The best way of overcoming this problem is to ensure that training courses correspond to the qualifications and stimulate the self-confidence of the unemployed (rather than making them compulsory). These courses should be of such quality and duration, that they can alter the marginal position of disadvantaged groups without adding to their distress.

Unfortunately, empirical evidence on the needs and aspirations of these groups relating to labour market provisions is very scarce. It is therefore recommended that policy makers at different levels should invest in studies on these issues. What follows is scraped together from scarce publications, and even to some extent a summing up of commonplaces.

Training is generally considered as an investment with uncertain outcome. The 'costs' of this investment on the part of the unemployed may be threefold:
- direct material constraints, like the financial cost (transport, child care, material, ...) or simply the absence of such facilities;

- indirect financial costs: participants have to postpone or reduce their job search activities while they attend courses and hence are increasing their expected unemployment spell. If courses are not of sufficient quality and duration to improve their qualifications, they may even have a negative employment effect. Policy-makers should acknowledge that neither the direct material costs, nor the indirect costs can be borne by poor participants: in other words, adequate remuneration of participants is an essential condition for success;
- it is also necessary to remove the psychological constraints, in order to enable unemployed people to participate in programmes and achieve good results. Some studies suggest that tackling some of the psychological aspects of unemployment through social assistance and pastoral care may help unemployed people into employment faster than those without that help. The same holds for participation in labour market programmes: obstacles such as a negative self-image, fear of failure, threat of exclusion, fatalism and so on should be removed by linking provisions with social assistance using a holistic approach. Additionally, positive support seems to be a better incentive than pressure and sanctions.

The qualifications offered should also correspond to the *needs of the labour market*. If for some courses the general experience is that participation does not help (re)employment, it is rational not to participate. Therefore it is necessary to give unemployed people realistic information about employment possibilities and the needs of the local labour market. This can be done through guidance and orientation courses. However, it has to be admitted that diagnosing the 'needs of the labour market' is very difficult.

For some of the most disadvantaged unemployed (older, totally unskilled, long-term unemployed) training is not necessarily the best strategy to start with. When the expected return to training is lower - e.g. for reasons of age or former school failure - or when the financial need is so urgent that it does not allow for postponed incomes, *direct employment* seems to be a better response in the short run, possibly supplemented by training in a second stage. This justifies the strategy of many local employment initiatives, sometimes called 'social economy projects', which give priority to (non-profit) employment over training. We will turn back to this issue in chapter 6.

Stated more generally, the typologies of needs and motivations quoted in this chapter underline the importance of *differentiating* provisions, taking account of age, unemployment history, previous education and training, household situation, financial needs and so on. Besides formal (initial and advanced) training, other successful strategies may be job search courses, intensive guidance, on-the-job training, temporary work experience projects, direct employment, and even in some cases - why not ? - formal schooling. Reintegration of disadvantaged people into the labour market should moreover be considered as a *process* where they can receive a *combination* of services.

At-risk groups need to have easy access to programmes at an early stage of unemployment thus avoiding a cumulation of long-term unemployment with other handicaps. There are good examples of programmes that attempt to meet the needs of disadvantaged job-seekers and the labour market, through a good concept of training or employment and a strong partnership between employers and educators.

Notes

[1] The negative employment effects are explained by the fact that unemployed individuals postpone or reduce their job search activities while they attend the courses; apparently this is not offsetby a shorter expected duration of unemployment after the end of the courses.

[2] In this study De Witte confronts a representative sample of LTU with LTU participating in specific programme, the 'Weer-Werk Actie' ('Back-to-work action'), for LTU.

[3] In Belgium, a similar time table is drawn for the participant in 'Weer-Werk-Actie' ('Back to work action'). The participants of this programme were also satisfied with the time table.

[4] VDAB = Vlaamse Dienst voor Arbeidsbemiddeling en Beroepsopleiding (Flemish Employment and Training Agency).

5 The equity-efficiency dilemma

5.1 Introduction

Public-sector initiatives created to help the disadvantaged sections of society are often based on implicit paradoxes that can lead to a conflict between the equity of a measure and its efficiency. Moreover, the greater emphasis public employment service officers place on the efficiency of the schemes they run, the more the people being targeted tend to be excluded from the schemes. A good many training measures for the underprivileged have distorting effects of this type, particularly if their avowed aim is job placement or improving skills, which are quite logically the most common aims of employment policy measures.

It is proposed in this chapter to consider as a starting case the findings of a study carried out to assess the performance of the AIF (Actions d'Insertion et de Formation - Integration and Training Measures) initiative. This study, completed in 1991 on behalf of the Délégation à l'Emploi (Employment Delegation) and the Mission Interministérielle Recherche et Expérimentation (MIRE - Inter-Ministerial Mission for Research and Experiment) in France, analyses how the measures were applied in five departments: Isère, Lot-et-Garonne, Nord, Paris and the Vosges (Verdié and Sibille, 1992).

Then, we will compare these results with programmes in other European countries.

5.2 A qualitative analysis of the French AIF-scheme

5.2.1 Background to the AIF initiative

The AIF initiative, established in 1990, was much more streamlined and coherent than previous training initiatives which had been established one after the other for the unemployed. The initiative was targeted specifically on the long-term unemployed and within this category, those designated as priorities were: people who had been out of work for a very long period of time (more than three years), the over-50s and people in unstable situations, such as those in receipt of a minimum income allocated for integration purposes (RMI).

This increasingly specific targeting exercise was aimed at reaching the 'hard core' of the long-term unemployed category, including people who were unable to get into the labour market, even in times of economic growth, and who found it very hard to gain admittance to initiatives designed to combat unemployment.

Within the context of the Employment Programme the AIF initiative set its sights on two objectives. The idea was to:
- focus the social cohesion and integration-related schemes on the worst cases of social exclusion;
- raise the standard of professional skills and combat labour market selectivity.

The study showed that attempts to meet the first objective, ensuring equity, were often made to the detriment of the second one, promoting efficiency, and that public service officers tended to look for efficiency rather than equity.

5.2.2 'Creaming off' the candidates

The impact of this initiative is dependent to a large extent on the departmental authorities, and more specifically on the administration responsible for labour and employment (Directions départementales du travail et de l'emploi) and the employment agency (Agence nationale pour l'emploi) running the initiative. According to the research findings, the people participating in the measure had, during its first year of application, a higher than intended level of qualifications, in spite of significant differences from one department to another. The people with the most pressing needs are represented very unevenly and always less than their actual proportion in the long-term unemployed group. For example, no more than 5 to 10% of 'over-50s', in the five departments covered by the study had participated in an AIF initiative, even though they accounted for 27% of the long-term unemployed. Similar figures are reported for the other target groups.

Conversely, there was quite a large percentage of people not officially entitled to benefit from the initiative, mainly because they have not been out of work long enough, who did participate. From this point of view, the most dynamic department in the study involved the greatest number of people who should have been disqualified from the initiative because they had been registered for too short a time with the employment office (51.8%, or one in two). It also had the lowest percentage of 'over-50s' (5%) and the highest proportion of qualification-based courses (for more than half of the trainees). It is clear that these figures are all related to each other: the more people in difficulty that are admitted to the training courses (the main target of the measure), the harder it is to offer training that leads to real qualifications. The department in question, regarded as being the most dynamic one in the region as regards the implementation of the AIF initiative, has clearly put the emphasis on effectiveness (qualifications and possible job placement) to the detriment of even-handedness or equity. Trainees participating in the initiative are selected by a sort of 'creaming-off' process.

Explicit criteria used by public employment service officers

Some of the selection criteria used by public employment service officers may be described as explicit (the implicit criteria being discussed in the next subsection). As for the department in question here, the officers claim their selection procedures are based on:
- efficiency (priority is given to people who are motivated and have a goal in mind, as they are thought to be able to derive maximum benefit from a scheme). Or then again when the officers choose people from the short-term unemployed category, they feel they are helping the people to avoid 'joining the army of long-term unemployed later on';
- recruitment difficulties;
- 'humanitarian' reasons: it would be impossible not to allow someone to participate in a scheme on the grounds that he has not been out of work long enough.
Another possible criterion, one that is less explicit, is based on the fact that the AIF initiative includes on-the-job training and the credibility of the employment service officers is at stake among the companies

whom the officials might need to propose candidates to later on (this primarily concerns the employment offices). It is therefore tempting to select trainees who are most likely to be employable, who already have some skills and have not been out of work for too long a period.

Training bodies that are awarded the 'quality clause' by the public employment service are entitled to larger subsidies and sometimes the clause is conditional upon and directly linked to the number of trainees that find a job after completing a scheme. It is obvious, then, that this criterion does not encourage the training bodies, who in many instances select the trainees themselves, to pick unemployed people who are the most disadvantaged and those who have been out work for the longest periods of time.

Implicit classifications of unemployed people by the employment service officers are likely to increase selectivity

According to the study, the selection procedure is also affected by the fact that there is very little in the way of a real 'demand' for training among the long-term unemployed, particularly as this group of people tends to include the most underprivileged and people with the most difficulties (see chapter 4). As a lot of people suffering from exclusion failed to do well at school, they are frightened of finding themselves in a similar situation once more. Further, training schemes are often considered to be a dead end, more of a cul-de-sac than a highway to the labour market. The most frequent demand is for a job. When conducting their interviews, public employment service officers will have a tendency to try to pinpoint a training 'need' and to get the potential trainee to accept it, in other words, they will try to 'promote' this demand. This situation is far from fair, for the public-sector officer is aware of all the types of courses on offer, whereas the potential trainee is not. A priori, the latter is not much in favour of training and the path he takes will depend on the goodwill of the public service officer he meets.

Because the demand for training is rarely clear and explicit, the public service officer has to apply his own criteria when deciding what the needs are. 'Motivation' therefore becomes of paramount importance. Officials questioned by the researchers interpreted 'motivation' to mean sincerity, and a determination to improve one's situation. From this concept of motivation emerge implicit categories of 'good' or 'bad' unemployed people, with the 'goodies' being those that seem more prepared than others to invest in training, those who appear to be 'employable in the short term', and so on. It is clear that these categories, whether they are explicit or not, can only increase the selective nature of the initiative.

5.2.3 A selective training provision

The public service officers' assessments of how motivated a candidate is will of necessity have some effect on the proposal made to the potential trainee, because the AIF initiative may be based on schemes to do with rebuilding self-confidence, with integration, or with courses that do not lead to qualifications. In other words, a range of training schemes that differ in their effectiveness as to job placement. Of course, as the AIF initiative is supposed to be a customised one, there is a need to guide trainees in the light of their level of skills and of their needs, and this has to be seen as a positive factor. However, because the concept of 'motivation' is to a large extent subjective, public service officers will, in a bid to ensure efficiency, tend to steer people they think are less 'motivated' towards integration or confidence-rebuilding courses, ones that do not lead to qualifications, and are most distant from the labour market.

The researchers also report that in certain departments there is an excessive growth of integration or confidence-rebuilding courses, and particularly of assessment activities. The latter account for up to 70% of the training activities in one of the five departments covered by the study (as seen, this figure is a lot lower, when the short-term unemployed are represented in greater numbers). Admittedly, people who have been out of work for a long time need to get their bearings, assess their capabilities, their shortcomings and their potential. But the researchers are inclined to think that the emphasis on assessment in the AIF initiative might also have had something to do with the relative ineffectiveness of the training bodies in catering for the long-term unemployed. They are also inclined to have their doubts about the efficiency of the assessments, which are likely to be repeated at the start of each new training scheme, concerning job placement.

5.2.4 Lessons from the AIF experience

"The spirit of the initiative is geared towards placement and employment, although its participants have the least opportunities and the priorities are determined in relation to handicaps. The rate of job placement is looked upon by the training bodies as a constraint, but it is mainly through the trainee selection process that the job placement

---

opportunities can be enhanced" (Verdié and Sibille, op. cit.). In short, the more the initiative attains its first objective of increasing social cohesion for the benefit of the most disadvantaged, the less it achieves the second one of increasing the level of skills and reducing the selectivity of the labour market. This may have something to do with the association of the two objectives, which are difficult to reconcile during an economic downturn, when jobs are harder to find, at least through training schemes. At the very least, there would seem to be a need to ensure that the rate of job placement at the end of a course is no longer used as the main yardstick for assessing the standard or the success of a training scheme. It is a lengthy process training the disadvantaged so that they are in a better position to enter the labour market. Given the current situation, it is difficult to see how public service officers can be encouraged to enable the priority categories to gain admittance to training schemes and how training bodies can be induced to offer effective and innovative schemes, while continuing to use the job placement yardstick as an indicator of how relevant the courses are.

5.3 A general tendency ?

The scheme was only in its early days then; the study conducted in 1991 dealt with the findings of 1990. Nonetheless the results from 1992 show that these trends have not really disappeared from the AIF.

One notices first from the 1992 results that progress was made in the integration of target groups in the AIF: priority for the very long term unemployed was further reinforced, since they represented almost a quarter of all entries, compared with the global share of long term unemployed which remained stable (nearly two thirds of the total). On the other hand, the share of non-priority groups (less than 12 months of unemployment) remained large: 42% of the number of trainees in 1992, 45% in 1991. The explanation for this is the wish to prevent long-term unemployment for people faced with recurrent unemployment or placement failures. Nonetheless that means less places for priority groups.

Also, one sees a rise in the qualification level of trainees. The non-qualified now only represent 39% of the total (41.5% in 1991), as opposed to 43% for the CAP-BEP levels[1] 1 (42% in 1991) and 18% for the baccalaureate level and beyond (16.5%). This is due of course to the adjustment difficulties which the non-qualified are increasingly facing, but this in parallel increases the selectivity phenomenon when entering the scheme. Thus, innovative actions implemented in the field of industrial training involve a high proportion of trainees who do not belong to the priority groups (four out of ten): "the level required for entering a training scheme favours the better prepared of the applicants and more particularly the young" (Grézard, 1993).

One can assume that this perverse 'creaming effect' is a trend that is difficult to eradicate, since one can observe it in numerous schemes, in France and elsewhere.

Wuhl (1992) reports a similar development among the recipients of the individualised training credit (CFI = Crédit Formation Individualisé). The CFI, created in 1989 for the young unemployed and opened the following year to employees and in 1991 to adult job-seekers, is designed to make the training system more coherent by facilitating the use of individualised training itineraries, to validate the achievement and provide access to a job. According to Simon Wuhl, the CFI may offer indisputable benefits, but it does not prevent selectivity developing as regards access to modules 'at the top end of the range'. "The less disadvantaged groups of beneficiaries and recent school leavers gain access more quickly to the qualification-based stage of training and young people stay on the CFI scheme for only a short time. On the other hand, in spite of the improvements mentioned, the most disadvantaged group is more often estranged from the more qualification-based courses (...). The risk of going adrift remains: in time, the better educated young people entering the CFI scheme will tend to take up permanently all the room on the qualification-based training courses and the rest will be relegated to ever-longer itineraries".

The 'Viveret-report' on the RMI (Revenu minimum d'insertion) in France points at a similar problem. It mentions the 'iron laws of the labour market' and the need for credibility of the reinsertion services as main causes of the creaming-off effect.

5.3.1 Belgium

Obviously the phenomenon is not typically French. As already described in chapter 3, in Belgium, numerous employment initiatives ring-fenced at the outset for people recognised as being 'officially' unemployed, have recently been opened up under pressure from non-governmental organisations, to those receiving minimum benefits. However, it now seems that the recipients of minimum benefits are routinely being deleted from unemployment registers after three months, for 'administrative reasons'.

Also in Belgium, the national employment and training agency ONEM, now regionalised, has witnessed the same tensions between equity end efficiency. Maroy (1988, 1990) describes how the emphasis in the training supply of the agency has gradually shifted from social to economic objectives, but also how these conflicting sets of objectives are reflected in the structure of the provisions and in the working styles of the staff members. He attributes this tension mainly to the bipartite administration of the employment agency by the social partners: employers tend to put more emphasis on the economic targets, trade unions on the social objectives.

Following the interprofessionnal agreement in Belgium, 0.30% of the wage bill is spent to 'the integration of categories at risk'. 0.10% is used to fund the 'Guidance plan' of the government, 0.05% for day care provisions for children, and 0.15% can be used either within the sector for special projects, or as a contribution to the national 'Employment Fund' for projects under government supervision.

Very little is known about the actual use of the sectoral initiatives. However, it is interesting to note how the notion of 'categories at risk' has progressively been broadened, due to the unwillingness (mainly of employers) to encompass really marginalised groups.

- First collective agreement, 1989-1990 (0.18% of the wage bill): unemployed aged over 50, minimum income receivers, LTU (+ one year), women re-entering the labour market after three years of interruption, low-qualified unemployed (at most secondary education), youngsters in part-time (vocational) education, and handicapped jobseekers.
- Second collective agreement, 1991-1992 (0.25% of the wage bill): the same groups plus workers aged over 50 (threatened with collective layoffs, or with restructuring, or with the introduction of new technologies), positive action for female workers, some 'low-qualified' jobseekers with higher school degrees than LSE (in the banking sector, e.g. unemployed with no university degree are considered as low-qualified). Two-fifths of the 0.25% (0,10%) should be spent to the 'first generation' of risk groups (the 'weakest' groups).
- Third collective agreement, 1993-1994 (0.30% of the wage bill): the discretionary use of the 0.25% within the sectoral initiatives is reduced to 0.15%. (Another 0.10% is to be deposited in the national Employment Fund, and the remaining 0.05% - for child care services - in a fund for public provisions.) The target groups of that national Employment Fund are broadened ('almost LTU', female workers).

The 0.10%-quotum for the weakest groups (first generation) is suppressed and every sector decides on its own definition of risk groups. So, the risk of 'creaming off' for the weakest groups is more and more evident.

5.3.2 Denmark

In Denmark, jobs available in the private sector are mainly allocated to the best candidates in the long-term unemployed category. To some extent the process of creaming can also be observed in the social assistance system when it is decided who is going to get rehabilitation benefits (Gregersen, 1993). Most likely the same kind of creaming-off effect takes place on a smaller scale when the employment service is guiding the unemployed to make use of the education allowance for self-chosen education, or when social workers pick out clients in their follow-up procedures (Thaulow, 1990).

5.3.3 United Kingdom

In the UK, the large programmes of centrally funded training (Youth Training and Employment Training, now called Training for work) are delivered through Training and Enterprise Councils (TEC's and LEC's). Their funds are quite deliberately related to the 'output' they can deliver ('output related funding'), specifically qualifications and offers of employment; they are therefore implicitly encouraged to select and favour the better qualified/adjusted and spend less on the more excluded.

In February 1993, new contracts proposed by the government to TEC's were aimed to cut the length of training for the long-term unemployed (from 26 weeks to 14 weeks) while demanding that more of them are placed into jobs (the output related element averages 20%, the department wanted to raise this to about 40%). This time the employer-led bodies which deliver government training schemes in England and Wales said explicitly "they will be forced to 'cream off' those people most likely to get work or qualifications" (Lisa Wood, Financial Times 7 February 1993).

The UK Enterprise Allowance Scheme (EAS) was designed to assist the unemployed in setting up business by providing them with subsidies; it was evaluated by the Centre for Labour Market Studies; it concluded that the likelihood of success of the business created was influenced by the size of the financial investment made by the participants, putting it outside the scope of the great majority of the long-term unemployed. Also, those who had been unemployed for the shortest periods were most likely to succeed. The EAS was replaced in 1991 by the Business Start-Up Allowance (BSUA). An Analysis by the Unemployment Unit (Murray, 1994) shows how the scheme now helps many fewer people overall (only about a third of the number recorded in 1987). Within this reduced number, the share of the unemployed has decreased from 100% to 75%, with the share of long-term unemployed decreasing from 25% (in 1984) to 10% in 1991.

These changes are a result firstly of changes in eligibility rules, and secondly of the freedom given to TECs/LECs to be selective in how they target the scheme. The consequence has been that the scheme is now directed at improving the local economy rather than helping the unemployed. If viewed as an active manpower programme to help the unemployed, it is subject to a very high level of 'creaming off'.

Also in the UK, an interesting report analyses case studies in which employers took initiatives to recruit the LTU (Crowley-Bainton and White, 1990). This report shows that employers get involved in these initiatives mainly for their own economic interest (recruitment problems, rise in recruitment costs, high staff turnover) and not primarily because they feel socially responsible. This leads them inevitably to select people entering pre-recruitment schemes according to their employability. Nonetheless, an encouraging point is that the report underlines that, even if the motivations at the beginning are nearly always geared to increase efficiency for the firm, employers are often very pleased in the long term to have taken part in these initiatives, partly because of local publicity, but they also express surprise in the quality of the staff recruited. The long term unemployed became for them an unforeseen source of knowledge to which they gained access. This result seems to us particularly encouraging because it can represent an antidote to the stigma of long-term unemployment.

5.3.4 Luxembourg

In Luxembourg, the beneficiaries of the RMG (minimum guaranteed income), received, during the first years of implementation of that law, an introduction card to the employment services coloured differently from that of other job-seekers. Needless to say, this scheme proved to be highly discriminatory. It has in fact since been suppressed. Unfortunately, this has not totally suppressed discriminatory attitudes, and the creaming-off phenomenon among job-seekers depending on the RMG. "The truth is that beneficiaries of the RMG receive very few offers of interviews with a potential employer. (...) This is why it is very difficult to motivate them over the years to visit the placement offices when no serious offer is made to them" (Report on the RMG, Conseil supérieur de l'action sociale, 1993).

Two other recent measures have been taken - alongside other integration and training actions - for the beneficiaries of the RMG which can be considered to be closer to the labour market in terms of demands and allowances. They are the ATI (Affectation temporaire d'insertion, 1993) and work placements (1994).

The selection of beneficiaries is quite explicit in the these two measures, which are designed as a number of steps towards the labour market, depending upon the degree of employability of beneficiaries.

The ATI offers the recipients of the RMG, for whom it is considered that the 'link to a job cannot be re-established', 40 hours community work per week in exchange for an integration allowance equivalent to the minimum wage. The private company placements must be offered to 'the best performing' recipients carrying out community work, to give them the opportunity to get acquainted again with a private firm. Also, measures are planned to motivate employers to hire beneficiaries of the RMG, especially those 'who have demonstrated their abilities during the work placement' (excerpts from the above mentioned report).

Admittedly, selection procedures at the entry to a work placement are necessary, especially at the start of the scheme to ensure employer participation. But these different measures can be seen as a continuous selection process: the ATI are concerned with a relatively low-skilled group, work placements are for the more employable of them, and potential hiring for the best performing of the latter. The system could become rigid and could forbid entry to these more useful measures to any person not perceived as being work-ready. This is reinforced by an official document of the interministerial committee on social action of the Grand-Duchy (21 July 1993) which decided to "establish a distinction among the beneficiaries of the RMG between the work-ready and those who aren't. Only those considered to be work-ready must regularly visit the placement offices."

To sum up, one of the risks involved in initiatives for the disadvantaged is the tendency towards further labour market selectivity, at the expense of the need to promote social cohesion and equity.

5.4 Conclusions and policy implications

In conclusion, several points can be underlined with a view to improving the assessment (and indirectly, the design) of future measures as a way to diminish the creaming-off phenomenon.

To begin with, it seems paradoxical to present the short-term placement rate as the essential success criterion of measures targeted on the most disadvantaged groups. Effectively, these groups are often the most distant from the world of work, whether in terms of length of unemployment, of skill level, or of social handicaps. They are therefore the people who will have the greatest difficulties in obtaining a job through one single measure, requiring social assistance, tailored training measures, etc. To use the short-term return-to-work rate as a success criterion - and sometimes as a condition for supplementary resources, financial in particular - will almost inevitably lead training organisations and public services responsible for intake to use a strong selection process and thus creaming-off practices. This does not mean of course that the return to work has to be excluded as an objective for measures aimed at disadvantaged groups, but it is necessary to put this objective in a broader perspective in terms of evaluation of the relevance of the measure. This means also, in our opinion, that it is necessary to understand the reintegration of the most disadvantaged groups in a different way.

First, if placement rates are to be used to assess the effectiveness of an employment initiative, this has to be done not in absolute but in relative terms: in other words, in relation to comparison groups whose members have not benefited from the labour market initiatives in question, but who display the same characteristics as those who have.

There is evidence that the 'absolute' placement ratio may be seriously biased as a performance criterion applied to provisions for different target groups. One of the key conclusions of the assessment made to discover the impact of the European Social Fund's objectives 3 and 4 in Belgium (Nicaise e.a., 1995), was that initiatives targeted on the most disadvantaged groups are, when considered in 'absolute' terms, less successful in helping people back to work than other measures. However, in 'relative' terms (differences in placement rates between beneficiaries and non-beneficiaries with the same characteristics), the initiatives for disadvantaged people are highly effective and often more so than other kinds of measures (see also table A.4 in appendix 2, compare e.g. VDAB-prevoc.-training to VDAB-tertiary sector).

A recent French study on the effectiveness of employment policy initiatives draws similar conclusions. It also shows that the conditions governing re-entry into the labour market are always determined by how close the initiatives are to the business sector:
- 58-67% rate of employment three months after the application of various employment aid initiatives in the market sector;
- 50% for employment aid in the non-market sector for the CES (= Contrats emploi-solidarité). And these outcomes are new CES-contracts to a large extent;
- 26% and 33% for training courses (FNE-FI and AIF).

But it has to be borne in mind that these initiatives apply to different target groups, different market segments, and different strategies and forms of integration. In short, effectiveness rating should first of all involve assessing the employability of the recipients who are selected and guided, and use an approach that tends to reflect labour market mechanisms.

A more positive finding of the study is that in a comparison between beneficiaries and non-beneficiaries of the initiatives, in terms of the job placement rates for similar sections of the population, the long-term unemployed always score better when they have benefited from an employment measure. The likelihood of finding a job is considerably higher, up to 25 percentage points higher, for people with re-employment contracts (CRE = Contrats de retour à l'emploi), for example, compared to eight percentage points more for the AIFs). Employment policy initiatives also seem to have a positive effect in the case of unskilled young people (Aucouturier, 1993).

Besides their expression in relative terms (with comparison groups), genuine efficiency criteria should also involve a dynamic perspective. On the cost side, they should take into consideration, for the most disadvantaged groups, the length of time needed to gain access to the labour market, especially under difficult economic conditions. On the benefit side, on the other hand, one should take account of the fact that disadvantaged job-seekers (in the absence of intervention) are facing a longer expected duration of unemployment, and hence the expected return from placement is much higher for categories at risk than for the average unemployed. In other words, the placement of disadvantaged persons is worth more, in terms of public finance, than the 'easy' placement of job-seekers from stronger groups. From this perspective, the whole equity-efficiency dilemma as it is perceived so far by many policy makers and administrators in this area looks rather misguided or short-sighted. Haveman and Hollister (1991) and Gueron and Pauly (1991) review empirical evidence that in most cases supports this statement.

Some examples noted in this chapter suggest that in assessing measures for disadvantaged groups it is very difficult to isolate the effect of one single measure. People in disadvantaged groups often need a set of measures: guidance, social assistance, training, integration activities and work placements, in order to regain self-confidence, and to acquire the skills and qualifications needed to re-enter the labour market. It seems therefore important to us to implement schemes that facilitate and organise longer integration processes, which combine a set of measures and render more flexible and efficient the cooperation between the different partners involved. This is the case for example of the PLIE in France (PLIE = Plans locaux d'insertion économique - Local economic integration plans) whose aim is to increase the efficiency of the whole set of human, operational and financial means for fighting unemployment in a given area. The PLIE are co-financed by the ESF. This approach makes it possible to assess the results according to the return-to-work criteria of the whole of the scheme, instead of each measure being taken in isolation.

Finally, it is worth giving a more sustained look at the involvement of companies in the measures aimed at disadvantaged groups. Of course, the world of private sector companies and the one of integration of disadvantaged groups have very different ideas about what is important. But there are European examples of innovative projects implemented in partnership with, or by, companies. It is necessary to publicise these examples of good practice to motivate other companies to get more involved in integration schemes. In one of the British examples mentioned above, companies engaged in employment initiatives for the long term unemployed prove to be durably satisfied and have been surprised by the quality of the person hired. A strong publicity on results of this type could have an impact on too harsh selection procedures of beneficiaries, since we have seen that creaming-off phenomena were the more frequent when companies were involved in these measures.

Notes

[1] CAP = certificat d'aptitude professionnelle; BEP = brevet d'études professionnelles.

6 Dead ends, carousels and stigma effects

6.1 Introduction

Over the last 10 years or so strategies for combatting unemployment by means of targeted insertion measures have tended:
- to decentralize initiatives and programmes focussed on the unemployed; and
- to target integration programmes and training resources more explicitly at particularly disadvantaged groups.

In the Netherlands, public employment agencies were decentralized a few years ago. In the United Kingdom, many major public training courses and manpower programmes are administered on the local level by TECs and LECs, since 1991. Denmark started in 1994 to decentralize all existing schemes concerned with labour market policies. In Luxembourg, both the trend of decentralization of measures and of targeting on disadvantaged groups are best illustrated by the minimum income law (RMG) from 1986: within the framework of the RMG law a number of social services offering insertion programmes specifically to unemployed MIG-receivers have been created. While the general framework of existing insertion measures is established by law and coordinated by a central public administration, the actual measures are designed and delivered by local (private) organizations. The same decentralization process is foreseen within the French minimum income scheme (RMI): in this case, insertion programmes are designed and delivered on a regional level.

The private non-market sector has played a large part, together with local authorities, in promoting local initiatives and in some countries it has acted as a major catalyst for the development of specific programmes in favour of more vulnerable groups.

The decentralization of the efforts and resources in projects aimed at combatting unemployment may have made it possible in many cases to differentiate the provision and to respond in a more effective way to the needs of the more vulnerable groups of unemployed. Nonetheless, developing local initiatives does not provide a definite guarantee against dead ends, further stigmatization, and disqualification of participating job-seekers. On the contrary, a key hypothesis in this chapter is that the decentralisation and targeting tendencies imply, to some extent, a risk of reproducing the existing segmentation of the labour market, by orienting the most disadvantaged candidates to sidetracks which in one way or another do not lead to the regular labour market.

In order to simplify the analysis, we will first concentrate the analysis on the training market (section 2); thereafter we will extend it (much more briefly) to local employment initiatives (section 3) and other types of measures (section 4).

6.2 Sidetracks and dead ends in training provisions

6.2.1 Segmentation of training provisions

A clear distinction between pure training programmes and other insertion projects with a broader range of activities (community service, on-job training, skills development, business skills training, job-search skills training, and job-creation programmes, ...) is not always easy, as many projects which do not explicitly nor exclusively focus on training may include implicit elements of training. All schemes, including some training elements, are considered within this subsection.

Depending upon the types of providers and beneficiaries, three separate categories of training programmes on offer may be distinguished:
- training and skill updating programmes provided in the main by employers or social partners;
- training programmes designed for job-seekers and carried out under the supervision of the public authorities (national, regional or local);
- training programmes prepared and managed by the private non-market sector ('local initiatives', 'NGOs', etc.), sometimes also by local public welfare centres.

The first type of programme is provided mainly so as to enable employers to update the occupational skills of their employees and thus provide businesses with a means of meeting changing market requirements. These training schemes are in the main geared solely towards labour market requirements and they might involve initial training schemes (provided to people that have been recruited or are due to be recruited later on), continuing training schemes or retraining schemes. They are organised by social partners (employers, trade unions, professional chambers) and in certain cases are provided by private organizations or in cooperation with the public authorities, the role of the latter being to encourage and to coordinate the organization and delivery of the programmes.

The second type of programmes fits in with national and public strategies for combatting unemployment. They are often developed by the public authorities as a result of a legislative initiative, and are generally funded from the public purse or unemployment insurance funds. These training programmes may be addressed to job-seekers of all types or may form part of specific policies targeted upon particular categories; older job-seekers, the long-term unemployed, young people without work, returning women, and so on. One of the key objectives common to all these programmes is the need to achieve some correspondence between the job-seeker's level of qualifications and the labour market requirements (of employers) for qualifications and occupational skills. This second type of programmes has a wider focus than the first one in the sense that the characteristics of job-seekers are taken into account.

The third type is conceived and carried out by the non-market sector. The programmes of this type are said to differ from the first two types by their scale and their geographical scope (local projects in the main - the non-market sector takes pride in underscoring its ability to react flexibly and creatively to local needs), their funding methods (joint, with or without the participation of the national and local public or Community authorities) and above all by often being targeted upon specific categories of job-seekers, generally regarded as particularly vulnerable or liable to social exclusion (the disabled, young people who have left home, people on social benefits, the homeless, migrants and ethnic minorities, the mentally ill, (former) drug addicts, people who have been in prison, and so on). More often than not, the training offered by these programmes is primarily a reflection of a need pinpointed in certain specific categories of job-seekers. This contrasts with the public-sector programmes which are geared more towards the sort of qualifications required by the labour market. This different view-point often induces the non-market sector to provide, in addition to qualification-oriented training, an array of extra services such as individual guidance and counselling, housing facilities, and help in combatting discrimination by society in the broadest sense of the term.

Without wishing to overlook the existence of joint training programmes in which public authorities and local associations are both involved in the same initiative, nor programmes carried out in partnership with employers, and without wishing to minimise the importance of the training provided by employers in a drive to maintain and create jobs, in the rest of this chapter we will - just for simplicity's sake - make a comparison between the 'mainstream' - mainly public - schemes, on the one hand, and the 'alternative', mainly private local projects, on the other.

At present, the only means of examining (in the light of the literature available) the differences between the different types of training (public and private) and local employment initiatives on offer to vulnerable groups is to pose questions. In the sequel to this research project an attempt will be made to illustrate the differences with practical examples culled from the countries taking part in the joint project.

Consideration will be given to the main objectives, the recruitment and selection procedures, the funding arrangements, curricula, operating procedures and, last but not least, the outcomes of the provisions. As concerns training provisions, attention will be focused on public versus private initiatives.

6.2.2 The professed objectives

An analysis of five case studies of training projects for the long-term unemployed carried out by HIVA (Nicaise e.a., 1990) shows that the background of the initiators determines in large part the (professed) objectives of a project.

- Community development agencies stress social emancipation objectives. The training programmes are not primarily oriented to the job market but aim more at helping participants break out of social isolation, restore their self-esteem and release a new dynamism: the first objective is not 'to fill a gap in the job market', but their offer is focused much more on 'what the participants are capable of'.
- Public training is more oriented towards the economy. The main objective is to combat unemployment as efficiently as possible by meeting an explicit demand for workers in a specific sector.

- Schemes set up by the unemployment organisations and the labour unions combine both objectives, the social ones as well as the economic ones.

A study in Luxembourg within the PETRA programme (Wagner, 1990) concerning 3 public and 4 private projects offering training facilities for young unemployed again shows that the primary aim of public training schemes is to offer unemployed people opportunities for acquiring qualifications that are of a better standard and more in line with current labour market requirements and thus to increase their chances of getting back to work. The selection mechanisms, financial resources, equipment and strategies are made conditional upon this primary objective.

Projects conducted by the non-market sector are likely to have a wider aim with the activities involved seeking to minimise social exclusion in all its aspects. Thus, while striving to boost the occupational capabilities of trainees and making it easier for them to find work, the projects also seek to offer help in finding accommodation, paying off debts, solving personal and family problems (including personality development), combating discrimination, and so on. The time, energy and resources available have to be shared out to try to meet the numerous objectives, and sometimes to the detriment of the training itself.

6.2.3 Recruitment and selection procedures

As a primary consequence of the specific objectives of each sector, public and private schemes do not have the same target groups: analyses of the target groups and of actual groups of participants in the Member States show that in countries where public and private programmes exist, they are targeted upon different groups of unemployed people.

Both are concerned with job-seekers, but in the case of those taking part in public projects, the major (and sometimes only) problem with the participants is likely to be that their qualifications are unsuitable for the current labour market requirements; whilst participants in projects run by the private non-profit sector not only lack suitable qualifications and occupational skills but also often have several personal and social handicaps: a 1993 report from HIVA comparing the NGO and public offer of prevocational training (Eloy and Nicaise, 1993) illustrates clearly that NGO's reach many more uninsured job-seekers and people with multiple problems (lack of qualification, poor health, family problems, ...).

The new Foyer pilot projects in United Kingdom (a private pilot-scheme designed and provided by the YMCA[1]) are another illustration of a more specific targeting by private schemes onto the more vulnerable presenting a cumulation of disadvantages: the vast majority of the clients of the YMCA Foyer pilots are reported not to be job ready and in need of skills and training. Most Foyer clients are also seen to have special needs, for example relating to social skills, insecurity and lack of self-confidence. Hence, they are thought to require extra help beyond that of a normal Jobclub (Crook, 1994).

The reason for there being two different sets of clientele can be traced back to the different objectives and, secondly, to the implicit or explicit selection procedures of the public sector (which is good at providing participants with qualifications but not at offering social guidance). Maybe the private projects have had to compensate in a certain sense for these selection procedures by focusing primarily on the most disadvantaged groups. Formal selection procedures are often used by public programmes (such as having a minimum of work experience in one field, or having a minimum vocational qualification level, or having unemployment benefit (sometimes for a specific, minimum period). Among the 5 case studies carried out by HIVA in 1990, the only public scheme under study was also the only one using a formal selection procedure, based on psychological and medical tests. In the private projects, by need or by choice, there is very often an implicit or explicit positive discrimination towards the less advantaged job-seekers (weak job experience, low levels of education and training, people without unemployment benefit or with poor (no) social protection, people facing personal difficulties, ...).

In Belgium, Luxembourg and presumably elsewhere in Europe, the group of unemployed without unemployment benefit or without full social assistance is largely excluded from public employment and training provision. This is one of the reasons for the importance of those private schemes, which do reach this public.

On the other hand, not all public programmes are confined to more employable job-seekers, they may also be targeted explicitly at vulnerable groups:
- in Denmark, AMU courses are directed to both the vulnerable groups (immigrants, LTU, ...) and to employees. However, the very high demand for these courses means that most disadvantaged groups in the labour market are left out;

- in Luxembourg, public training centres for the employed (continuing training) and the unemployed are also open to MIG-receivers, but first evaluation results show that drop out and non-placement to the labour market are the rule for this particular group of participants.

Recruitment channels may also be different in the two types of schemes. In the Belgian study (Nicaise e.a., 1990), public employment agencies and public welfare agencies play a major role for both the public and the private schemes whereas community development projects themselves are important providers of participants to their own schemes. In Luxembourg (Wagner, 1990), recruitment channels are separated: participants in public schemes are mainly provided through national public agencies (employment agencies and school orientation services provided 72% of all participants) whereas most participants in the private schemes have been sent to the projects by local public and private social services (57%).

6.2.4 Funding

Projects may also be differentiated through their funding. At this level, the total volume of resources is a first element to be looked at, but beside the total budget available, other factors with respect to funding are important: projects may be differentiated by how secure their financial support is and by how frequently payments are made. These factors are likely to influence long-term planning, the widening of existing activities (in response to increasing needs) as well as the development of new activities (in response to new needs).

As mentioned, public training projects are generally funded through budgetary means or through financial resources managed and controlled by the public authorities and as a result it is often possible to plan long-term and wide-scale projects. In certain cases, the resources may be boosted for a short while, if the political decision-makers should deem this necessary (for example, in the wake of a sharp increase in the rate of unemployment, the decision-makers might agree to vote in favour of a special funding package, allow a temporary reallocation of public funds or accept the need to breach budget ceilings).

When considering the projects being conducted in the non-market sector, it is clear that, typically, less money is available: according to the case studies made by HIVA in Belgium (Nicaise e.a., 1990) local NGO's, which mainly reach the most vulnerable groups of job-seekers, seem to suffer from a constant lack of financial resources. In Luxembourg, as in Belgium, local (private) projects tend to offer multiple services to the

---

most vulnerable groups. Most of these projects have financial support from different administrations, and in a few cases from local authorities. In general, support from government is given in the form of a grant to be negotiated and renewed each year, but this support does not automatically cover all costs, so that most projects are forced to find some alternative financial resources (mainly when trying to enhance their provision or when developing new activities).

More important sometimes than insufficient funding can be insecure and irregular funding (resulting from precarious contracts with public authorities), which makes it difficult to make any long-term plans or react quickly in the event of an increased demand on the part of the job-seekers. Late or irregular funding is a difficult problem which most private local schemes have to face. Delays with money transfers to local projects cofinanced through Community programmes may illustrate this: numerous projects have been obliged in the past to rely on pre-financing by local, regional or national authorities or to fall back on expensive bank credit while waiting for the money to arrive.

In projects facing financial difficulties, project managers tend to devote too much energy (in terms of time and personnel) looking for sources of funding and trying to get spending under control: "the private projects have to scrape together whatever they can in the hope that they can find something to keep them going for a time" (Nicaise e.a., 1990). One of the main suggestions from this HIVA-report is to emphasise the need for greater financial security and institutional stability for private schemes.

Thus, against the backdrop of long-drawn-out economic recession leading to stringent budgetary policies, there is every reason to believe that the public authorities' (financial) participation in training projects developed by the non-market sector could soon be decreased. The difficulties met by the 'Stiftung Berufliche Bildung' from Hambourg (Glücklich and Boutez, 1993) resulted from sudden cuts and changes in subsidising policies: the project was offering (vocational) training facilities to over 1,000 disadvantaged unemployed. Following the cuts to subsidies to private schemes, 40 trainers were made redundant; moreover, modular qualification developed and delivered over a long period was no longer possible, due the newly fixed maximum duration of vocational training within subsidised schemes. Both the participants and small enterprises in the region (hiring large numbers of participants who received appropriate qualifications) suffered losses by this action.

6.2.5 Operation of the programmes

Related in part to the objectives, to the characteristics of participants and to the funding arrangements, the operating procedures for projects conducted in the non-market sector are also likely to prove to be somewhat precarious.

A first aspect to be examined is the level of qualification of staff. Qualification of trainers and teachers is likely to have an influence on the results: following a CEDEFOP report on continuing education and training of the long-term unemployed in ten Member states of the EC (Otte and Schlegel, 1992) "even if information on the qualifications of the staff is lacking, there nevertheless seems to be a trend towards higher success rates in projects showing a larger potential of higher qualified staff".

In terms of staff, public operators can boast the advantages of qualified and experienced instructors (in general, trainers within public schemes meet the qualification requirements for trainers and teachers in the public school system), whereas trainers in private schemes do not always have these qualifications. Personnel costs are such a heavy burden for private promotors, that often use is made throughout of trainers in subsidised job schemes and volunteers. Underpaid staff, or staff having a precarious status are factors which are not likely to ensure professionalism and continuity.

In the public sector, a full range of up-to-date facilities is more likely to be found, as well as training syllabuses based on official programmes, with recognised qualifications at the end of the training. The latter have to be seen in relation to a possible monopoly of public administration for delivering official certificates - even if sometimes, like in the UK, there seems to be a considerable mistrust by employers vis-à-vis the whole qualification system.

While seeking for support from, or partnerships with employers, public projects again may have comparative advantages: formal contracts between national, regional or local authorities and employers, training allowances to participants, cofinanced programmes. On top of this such partnerships with employers imply concurrence with the needs of industry, opportunities for in-service training, landing a job at the end of training, and so on. In the PETRA sample from Luxembourg (1990), participants from public schemes actually were more often offered work experience in private companies (67%) during training than their companions from the private sector (32%). Private schemes tried to compensate for the lack of relations with employers from the market sector by creating their own enterprises (social economy initiatives).

6.2.6 Outcomes

As each type of provision serves different target groups, one can hardly expect them to yield similar results. In general, evaluation studies of the labour market effects of training show that training cannot compensate for differences in individual or group characteristics, even if it appears to be relatively more effective for disadvantaged groups. One illustration is the Belgian evaluation of training measures cofinanced by the ESF, summarised in table A.4 in appendix. The NGO projects yield placement rates, six months after completion of the scheme, of approximately 40%, compared to ratios between 65 and 80% for mainstream public schemes. All too often, such differences are attributed to a lesser quality of the private schemes; in reality they must be attributed at least partly to the disadvantages of the target group reached in these schemes. But, in the light of the foregoing analysis, the question remains whether or not the lower achievements of private local projects are affected by the poor circumstances in which they have to operate.

The CEDEFOP study on training projects for LTU (Otte and Schlegel, 1992) involved an interesting attempt to quantify the effectiveness of training and its determinants in an alternative way. A distinction was made, not between public and private provisions, but between projects targeted at particularly disadvantaged groups and others. When using placement rates as the only yardstick of effectiveness, the former indeed showed a much less favourable score: one third of the projects had a 'low' success rate, as opposed to 15% of the projects targeted on more qualified LTU. However, when some index of 'social reintegration' was added to the placement rate as yardstick of success, the gap between the two types of projects narrowed considerably (although without disappearing). Indirectly, this implies that the projects targeted at particularly disadvantaged LTU scored better with respect to social reintegration, whereas the other projects yielded better employment results. Thus, the differences in outcomes are not only quantitative but also qualitative.

These findings are in line with those of Eloy and Nicaise (1993), in that private projects appear to score better relating to psychological effects such as improved self-esteem, whereas the public scheme yield better labour market effects.

With respect to the pedagogical approach to training for the hard core of the long-term unemployed, the CEDEFOP study demonstrates that projects offering pastoral care alongside content-orientated technical training are much more successful in achieving their aims than projects offering purely technical training to the same target group (Otte and Schlegel, 1992). The authors thus pinpoint the potential strength of private projects, namely their 'holistic' approach, alongside their weaknesses.

As a conclusion, it must be recognised that it is an oversimplification to conclude that local NGO-projects targeted at the most disadvantaged groups achieve weaker results as a consequence of their poorer funding. The analysis rather seems to indicate that public and private provisions both have their strengths and weaknesses, and that their outcomes are qualitatively different. However, from the point of view of labour market policy, employment outcomes are the ultimately predominant evaluation criterion, and consequently, it would be preferable for the NGO-projects to score higher in this respect besides their social impact.

At the same time, the analysis suggests that there is a potential for more effective programmes if the strengths of both types of provisions could be combined. At present they rather seem to compete against each other in a segmented market, yielding sub-optimal results for the hard core of the unemployed.

6.2.7 Suggestions for further research

The hypothesis of a dual or segmented system of training provision in the Member States may be summarised by a two-axes diagram, taking account of the various factors involved (with the main focus on the objectives of the schemes and the characteristics of target groups):
- one axis referring to the categories within the public being targeted: a continuum between job-seekers whose main problem is a lack of suitable skills, on the one hand, and a group whose members not only lack skills but also have several personal and social disadvantages on the other;
- a second axis with on the one side job- and qualification-oriented projects and on the other individually-oriented ones.

This scheme is proposed for assessment later on as it makes it possible to categorise each project being examined by referring to its position on each of the two axes. The achievements can also be assessed in the light of a project's position on the diagram. The 'segmentation' hypothesis

---

would imply that most public projects are situated in the north-western quadrant, with qualification-oriented programmes skimming off the least disadvantaged job-seekers. The private non-profit training schemes would mostly belong to the south-eastern quadrant, with more disadvantaged participants, less directly work-oriented programmes and, as a consequence, poorer placement results. It would be interesting to verify to what extent projects in the south-western quadrant (i.e. working with disadvantaged groups but geared primarily towards qualification and employment) obtain better results than those in the south-eastern quadrant. This would help to answer the question of whether the observed segmentation is determined by supply or demand factors, and whether it can be overcome or not.

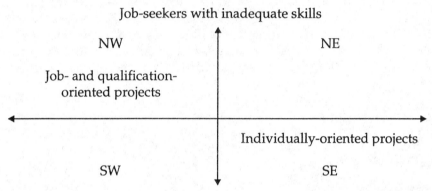

6.3 Side-tracks in local employment provisions

As in the previous section, an attempt will be made here to describe and analyse different approaches within a single reintegration strategy, focusing on potential side-tracks and dead-ends where the poorest could be 'dumped'. This time, the analysis will be focused on local employment initiatives instead of training; it will be much more tentative and succinct, as less empirical evidence is available at this stage.

The heading 'local employment initiatives' (also 'social enterprises' or 'social economy initiatives') covers a wide range of initiatives across Europe, such as the social co-operatives in Germany and Italy, the Enterprises d'apprentissage professionnel in Belgium, the Sociedades Anonimas Laborales and Casas de oficios in Spain, the 'enterprises d'insertion' in France, the 'sociale werkvoorzienings-bedrijven' (social

workshops) and 'banenpools' (job pools) in the Netherlands, the community businesses in Scotland, the task force initiatives in the UK.

These projects are significant for:
- being focused on the market economy, in other words they produce
  goods for the local market;
- deciding that their main goal should not be to turn a profit but to
  promote the 'common interest', and employment for disadvantaged
  groups in particular (jobs take precedence over capital);
- being able to follow other goals, such as environmental management,
  local services, etc.

For many unemployed people who are particularly underprivileged,
social enterprises are better suited to their requirements than are
training schemes. The advantages for these people are the less demanding approach of these businesses and the opportunities for individual
development on offer (see chapter 4).

6.3.1 Segmentation of local employment initiatives for disadvantaged groups

Needless to say, there is an enormous diversity of such initiatives. A
good survey of provisions and legislation in Europe can be found in
Carton and de Crombrugghe (1993). For our purpose, we would again
distinguish between three 'archetypes' of social enterprises:
- 'work experience initiatives' offering just a temporary job, often combined with on-the-job training, with a view to transferring the worker
  to the regular labour market within a well-defined time limit;
- 'social cooperatives' functioning on a quasi-commercial basis, whose
  aim is to create new and *permanent* jobs in a 'niche' of the market;
- 'social workshops' that work on a non-profit basis, offering permanently subsidised jobs to the least 'employable' job-seekers.

The first type of initiatives is found in France as 'entreprise d'insertion'
(EI), in Belgium as 'entreprise d'apprentissage professionnel' (EAP), or
in Spain as 'escuelas-taller'. They are mainly geared to disadvantaged
youngsters, sometimes also to the long-term unemployed or ex-
offenders. The temporary employment of these persons is aimed, on
one hand, to developing a number of work attitudes which were possibly lost as a result of a longer period of inactivity or personal problems; on the other hand, it helps to overcome stigma effects vis-à-vis
potential external employers by 'proving' the employability of the
candidate.

'Social cooperatives' start from the premise that the regular labour market excludes some categories of job-seekers although they are not necessarily unproductive. By developing an alternative business culture, based on human values rather than profit-making, they aim at reintegrating disadvantaged workers into an 'almost normal' job. In most cases these enterprises are subsidised, either degressively over time for every new employee, or in the form of a limited lump sum, or for staff subsidies. In this way an equilibrium is sought between sound economic management and compensating the handicaps of the target groups.

This is not the case with 'social workshops', that pretend to engage the hard core of 'very difficult to place' unemployed. Their employees are not believed to be able to move into a normal job ever again, due to personal problems, stigma or handicaps. Hence, they try to provide stable, permanently (and strongly) subsidised jobs. Examples of this type of enterprises are found mainly in the Netherlands (Sociale Werkvoorziening), Flanders (sociale werkplaatsen) and Germany.

Available literature shows that many of these new initiatives do actually provide an answer to local needs or allow for the creation of innovative organisational structures for reintegrating the less-favoured groups (qualitative success). In some cases, immediate return to the labour-market cannot be seen as the first aim of local projects. Dealing with a public facing multiple problems (health, housing, financial situation, family relations, social security status, psychological stability, unfitness for regular activity, ...), intermediate targets have to be set. In these cases, again in order to fight lack of personal perspectives and growing discouragement, links to more labour orientated projects or further training must be made.

Nonetheless, what does need criticising is the fact that in certain circumstances these fresh initiatives may conceal pitfalls and dead ends which further stigmatise and disqualify the job-seekers involved, thus lowering their chances of returning to (regular) work and helping to segment the labour market (into people who are 'employable' and those who are 'unemployable'). In the following discussion, we will throw a critical light on the ways in which vulnerable groups are sometimes 'trapped', especially into the latter type of employment initiative (social workshops), whereas otherwise they might move up to a more 'normal' job.

6.3.2 The economic viability of the projects

Sometimes, the primary economic goals of the projects cannot be achieved: the evaluation of the social workshops in Flanders (Vanhuysse and Henckes, 1992) shows that 9 out of 12 projects were not able, after covering fixed costs, working expenses and the wages of staff, to achieve any degree of auto financing of participant wages (in other words, their potential for self financing of participants' wages was zero or negative). Among the reasons for this financial debacle, the authors mentioned (besides the obvious handicaps of the target group) lack of experience and professionalism of initiators, a too small scale of operation, and a wrong choice of activities (weak market segments such as gardening, recycling, maintenance, ... see chapter 4). Very similar results were obtained in an in-depth study of 7 social workshops in Limburg (Van Meensel and Bogaert, 1992): on the costs side, this report revealed high hidden costs (in the form of staff paid on public employment programmes, free rent of buildings, voluntary work, ...), up to 50% of the visible costs on average; on the benefit side, the low average productivity was attributed to the same factors as those mentioned by Vanhuysse and Henkes (1992), in addition to the fact that some projects provided for on-the-job training of participants. Again, the potential for self financing of participants' wages was found to be negative in 4 out of 7 projects, and very low for two projects.

6.3.3 Status and job satisfaction of participants

Sometimes the work on offer gives little satisfaction (either in terms of money or in terms of the personal development of participants - this type of work is seen as a stop-gap until something better comes along), but the most significant thing, once again, is the lack of any real scope for finding a permanent job. Thus, the number of permanent jobs being offered to participants, with the sorts of guarantees and advantages associated with a standard employment contract (wage structure, affiliation to a social security system, guaranteed rights of workers), may remain less than expected, for the projects are not always able to do any more than propose temporary, subsidised and more or less informal work of a marginal type. When this is the case, involvement in these projects scarcely increases the chances of participants to improve their position, but what it would do is to cause those suffering from exclusion to lose heart and the experience would leave them with the impression that they have been wasting their time.

6.3.4 The outcomes

It may seem a little unfair to assess the outcomes of social workshops on the basis of 'transition rates' to the regular labour market, since the operators themselves aim to provide for permanent subsidised employment if necessary. Nevertheless, one can adopt a normative viewpoint and argue that as a rule, labour market integration cannot be accomplished in separate circuits of (pseudo-)employment, but requires stable, normally remunerated jobs fully covered by social security as a result, either within the projects, or on the regular labour market.

The in-depth evaluation of seven local initiatives in Flanders mentioned above (Van Meensel and Bogaert, 1992) showed how very expensive and highly subsidised 'social workshops' tend in reality to keep their employees busy in marginal activities, instead of putting them en route to the regular market. The self-reported 'success' rates of the projects (about 60% on average) are not time-related and include prolonged contracts within the projects as well as transition to training (the mirror image of this 'success rate' being drop-out or return to inactivity). The real transition rates are closer to 1/3 and were sometimes so disappointing that subsidies to some of the projects have been cut down as a result of the report. It also revealed that often very little effort was made by the projects relating to mediation and guidance.

6.3.5 Lessons for local employment initiatives

A full evaluation of this strategy would require - as with the training provisions discussed above - more extensive data collection, in order to make more precise comparisons between the different types or 'segments' of the local employment initiatives possible.

As a preliminary conclusion from the scarce data reviewed above, we try to list the following recommendations for a more effective approach:
- avoid the isolation of the most disadvantaged into separate provisions;
- set the (re)integration in the regular labour market as the ultimate goal for every person, even if this requires an indefinite time;
- draw up individual reinsertion plans, stipulating all steps to be taken as well as intermediate evaluation points;
- motivate participants by working conditions (including remunerations) as close as possible to standard contracts in the regular labour market;

- link work experience with formal and on-the-job training, tailored to the needs of every individual worker, and with mediation and guidance;
- train project promotors for effective entrepreneurship and provide specific business and advice services for social economy initiatives.

It goes without saying that these conditions of success can only be realised at a very high cost, which means that the public authorities have to invest sufficiently in these projects, but with the expectation of a higher long-term return than is the case at present.

6.4 Side-tracks and dead ends in other provisions

6.4.1 A general tendency ?

Besides training and local employment initiatives, numerous other examples can be given where separate schemes were set up for the most disadvantaged job-seekers, due to the failure of well-performing integration measures to include them.

Carton and de Crombrugghe (1993) report the example of the 'dualisation' of the provisions for school-fatigued youngsters attending part-time education. In chapter 4, the alternating education scheme was described as an example of good practice where social and economic objectives were reconciled through a strong commitment of both employers and schools. One drawback of the early experiments was that - in a context of mass unemployment - they failed to reach the most disadvantaged: pupils from broken families, with a low socio-economic background, and with the weakest school careers. This gave rise, in the French-speaking community of Belgium, to the creation of the EAP's (= Entreprises d'apprentissage professionnel) where these youngsters are employed in precarious jobs, without any social security insurance, without formal certification, and in the margin of traditional industries. A similar evolution was observed in Flanders, with the creation of so-called 'bridge projects', a kind of social workshop for transitory part-time employment (40 weeks) in renovation, gardening, etc. It quickly appeared to be the case that these projects were extremely expensive (due for a large part to staff expenses), showed high dropout rates and poor post-training placement results (Nijsmans and Nicaise, 1993).

Within the Luxembourg RMG scheme (= revenu minimum garanti), different insertion measures including training and community service are offered to MIG-receivers (with the participation of local projects).

As few transfers from these measures to the labour market have been registered, and as possible carousels have become more and more obvious, new instruments have been developed, mainly the 'temporary insertion contracts' (ATI = affectation temporaire d'insertion) which correspond to a 100% subsidised, 40 hours/week job offer within community service or in private companies. There are fears that here again participants will become stuck for some time with no realistic chance of being hired.

The 'Contrats emploi solidarité' (CES - solidarity for work) contracts represent one of the major instruments of labour market policies in France (600,000 contracts in 1992) offering half-time jobs for a limited time in the non-market sector (including a training offer in some cases) to the vulnerable unemployed (LTU, MIG-receivers, young unemployed with no vocational qualification, ...). While this instrument represents a first offer of integration to a large number of people suffering from social exclusion, it has to be noted that for a large group of the participants, this does not go beyond a temporary solution. CES contracts are followed in too many cases by a new period of redundancy. A regular work contract as a result of a CES contract is certainly not the rule.

The problem with the integration of disadvantaged groups in public employment programmes is also recognised in the Netherlands, namely in the 'labour pools' ('banenpools') for the LTU, as well as in the Flemish 'back to work' programme. In the present context of mass unemployment, temporary jobs in non-profit activities normally end with backsliding into unemployment, yielding at most a renewed contact with the labour market and a reactivation of job search activities. On the other hand, the discouragement at the end of the employment period is all the greater. A more extreme example are the newly created municipal odd-jobs services for the LTU in Belgium. These ALE (= agencies locales de l'emploi) provide for temporary part-time jobs (less than 40 hours per month) which are strictly confined to activities that do not compete with regular work: gardening, home maintenance, occasional administrative work in municipal or non-profit services, ... as a complement to the unemployment benefit. At the same time, these jobs do not seem to yield very useful experience nor stable prospects; rather they remove the participants from the ordinary labour market.

It would be worthwhile to examine whether such work experience programmes would yield more stable employment in the private sector. But in many countries there seems to be a reluctance on the part of policy makers to subsidise private employers in the profit sector for hiring disadvantaged job-seekers, mainly for fear of substitution and displacement effects. The more substitution and displacement, the fewer net additional jobs are created by a programme. (In the next chapter, the problem of substitution will be dealt with in greater depth.)

A new dilemma seems to emerge here, between 'additionality' and 'integration in the regular labour market'. The principle of 'additionality' of job creation programmes is indeed sometimes operationalised through the deliberate creation of separate employment circuits, well outside the regular labour market, but possibly with less perspectives for stable contracts. In the light of the foregoing analysis, this approach would need to be reconsidered: if 'additionality' implies further segmentation of provision, lower transition to regular jobs, and hence, less stable employment results, it would perhaps be preferable to accept more substitution. (Admittedly, our argument remains rather speculative and requires further investigation.)

6.4.2 Carousels

This refers to the idea that different arms of the administration may attempt to shift the responsibility for unemployed clients from one to another, as the desire to reduce their costs, reduce their degree of responsibility, or achieve administrative targets takes precedence over the needs of clients. This term also includes the phenomenon of clients completing, or just starting, one programme after another without their making any real progress in the labour market. It specifically does not include the good practice of people progressing through a number of programmes in a planned way because they have much headway to make before being able to participate in the labour market.

In Denmark there are examples of carousels in the Job Offer scheme, and arguably in the employment projects run by the municipalities where MIG-clients are employed just long enough to render them eligible for the (nationally funded) unemployment insurance scheme. As the income maintenance of the uninsured unemployed is expensive for the municipalities, some of the municipal provisions are used, not to integrate the unemployed, but to make them eligible to claim benefits from the insurance system. As soon as the unemployed become eligible, they are no longer entitled to benefits from the social assistance system. In this way part of the measures are managed for the sake of institutional interest, which results in the unemployed being pushed from one system to another.

In Belgium a similar carousel is thought to be the temporary work programme designed to move clients from social assistance back into social security (art. 60#7 of the law on social welfare centres). This is illustrated by some striking findings from an evaluation carried out by Van de Velde (1990); retrospective interviews with 173 individuals who had participated in the scheme three years earlier revealed that nearly all of them had indeed gained access to unemployment insurance. However, 91.5% had fallen back into unemployment immediately after the scheme; 61.4% were unemployed at the time of the interview, while 48.5% had remained unemployed for the whole three years following the scheme. Those who did fall back into long-term unemployment run the risk then of being excluded from unemployment insurance, and having to return on social assistance. Two important reasons for these bad results were the absence of training offers (only 5% had attended a formal training course) and the lack of guidance and mediation. As a consequence of these findings, the scheme was reorganised so as to include training and guidance for all participants. A second evaluation, 3 years after the reform (Wouters, Van Meensel and Nicaise, 1994) revealed that fewer participants (42%) had fallen back to persistent unemployment despite the economic recession of the early 1990s. In a third phase, the scheme was again improved by including intensive guidance and counselling services.

Observers in Denmark criticised the former system of unemployment insurance itself as being a carousel. The unemployed could stay within the unemployment insurance system for more than 10 years without having a 'proper' job. They did this by participating in the different offers they were entitled to receive from the Employment Service. Within the 10 year period the long term unemployed were obliged to participate in 2 job offers (each of 7-9 months duration) a training course (average duration 20 weeks), and a number of interviews at the Employment Service and at the Unemployment Insurance Funds. Critics argued that there a were too few incentives, especially for the most disadvantaged groups of long term unemployed, to break out of this system of income maintenance (Zeuthen, 1992). In this way the system itself, which has now been changed precisely in order to overcome these difficulties, was an obstacle to the labour market integration of the weakest groups of the unemployed.

In Luxembourg carousels are observed by workers in the field to exist, where they are termed 'social and training tourism', but there is little documented evidence and as always it is difficult to distinguish between individuals who need a series of programmes to fit them for

---

the labour market, and those who are spending their time on programmes as an alternative to employment in the labour market, either willingly or unwillingly. One analysis provided for this study shows that among young people taking part in initial vocational training in 1990, 30% had participated in one or more programmes before; and 60% had at least one job before with an average employment duration of more than 20 months. Only 24% of participants had had no work experience and no training.

6.4.3 Stigma effects

Job-seekers from disadvantaged groups nearly always have to face prejudice on the part of employers. A survey among Belgian employers (Ameels e.a., 1994) shows that each specific group of disadvantaged has to face specific prejudices endangering possible employment (young unemployed with low vocational qualification = lack of basic training; LTU = lack of motivation; returning women = time schedule conflicts; MIG-receivers = lack of personal stability, lack of motivation). We will talk about stigma effects, in the narrow sense, when hidden handicaps (MIG-receivers, people from poor socio-economic backgrounds, ex-offenders, ex-drug addicts, ...) are revealed to employers by the mere fact of 'benefitting' from a programme. Stigmatisation in the broader sense implies that 'visible' handicaps which are usually ascribed to a group (like long-term unemployment) are reinforced at the individual level by participation in a programme.

Following a study of Burtless (Dayton, Ohio, 1985) on the effectiveness of a targeted wage subsidy (intended to increase the employment of MIG-receivers by offering employers reimbursement for part of those worker's wages), job-seekers given experimental vouchers identifying them to employers as eligible for a generous wage subsidy were significantly less likely to find employment than were similar job-seekers without vouchers. Given the results of this study, poor employment effects as a result of a recent wage subsidy scheme (1993) for the elderly and the long term unemployed in Luxembourg (including MIG-receivers) should not be seen as temporary (mainly due to starting difficulties) only.

In Denmark, the mandatory training courses for long-term unemployed people in the framework of the job offer scheme have gradually got a rather bad reputation among employers (Aakrog e.a., 1991). Several reports emphasise this stigma effect as one of the reasons why the placement ratios after the training courses are so negligible (Madsen,

---

1992; Aarkrog e.a., 1991): not more than 13% of the participants appears to have a job within six months after leaving the course (Thaulow and Anker, 1992). According to Jensen e.a. (1992) the employment effects of the courses are even negative, compared with a control group of non-participants with the same profile. Similar results were obtained by Dolton, Makepeace and Treble (1993) for YT, the Youth Training scheme in the UK, which is a more or less mandatory scheme as well. If the results of these studies are correct, non-participation in the scheme would be a rational choice on the part of the individual, even if he/she would lose benefits, because (a) it would signal to employers that one is 'better' than the participants and (b) it would leave more time for job search. Other British studies (White and Mcrae, 1989) have pointed at the stigma effect of YT, but this has been alleged about many government-funded programmes in the UK.

A recent evaluation in Belgium (Vanroelen, 1993) shows that yearly transfers of the disabled from sheltered workshops (whose explicit aim - among other - is to get the disabled fit for the labour market) to regular jobs do not exceed 2%. As one of the possible reasons for this poor result, prejudice by employers against the lower work ethos and absenteeism in sheltered workshops, transferred to participants, are evoked. The argument is particularly relevant to non-disabled poor people who, by choice or by force, used to be sent to sheltered workshops as 'hard to place unemployed'. Fortunately, this practice has been abolished recently. In the Netherlands, however, both disabled and hard-to-place unemployed people are recruited in 'sociale werkplaatsen' (social workshops) that are, in fact, identical to sheltered workshops. This mixing of target groups is seen as harmful to both.

As we saw in chapter 5, stigma effects and prejudices against participants can be overcome by the elaboration of schemes ensuring commitment and active participation from employers from the start, as well as an efficient use of demonstration projects with good results and good publicity (which calls for a strong evaluation of projects, a serious follow-up of participants and an intelligent use of appropriate marketing strategies).

6.5 Conclusions and policy implications

This chapter, in contrast with the foregoing, has been mainly concerned with the problem of *effectiveness* in provisions for disadvantaged groups. It has mainly thrown a critical light on separate provisions, defined broadly as 'side-tracks', where the most vulnerable job-seekers are not necessarily integrated and even sometimes further disqualified. Our critical analysis should in no way be generalised to all special provisions; whereas it points at a number of pitfalls and inefficiencies, this certainly does not suggest that it would be preferable to throw away all local and/or targeted initiatives. On the contrary, our intention is eventually to improve their quality by identifying possible traps, as well as the ways to avoid them.

One should not forget that the tendency towards more decentralised and targeted provisions was inspired by the failure of general provisions to include the most marginalised job-seekers and to respond to local labour market needs. In chapter 4 we have pointed at some of these specific needs on the side of the target groups. The design of specific policies basically served three objectives, that are most worthy of consideration:
- to discriminate positively in favour of excluded and at-risk groups, where mainstream provisions fail to do so;
- to respond to specific needs (such as direct employment prospects for very low-skilled workers in a less competitive environment; literacy, general and initial training; social assistance, psychological support, ...);
- in some cases, a third objective was to counter substitution and displacement effects by developing new markets (the 'additionality' criterion).

The spectrum of inefficiencies reflected in our analysis - and due to the focus of our research - most probably overlooks a great number of positive results; on the other hand, it has perhaps the merit of identifying drawbacks and dangers at different levels. The illustrations reported in the text demonstrate that these dangers are not unrealistic nor exaggerated.

Three types of inefficiencies have been discussed:
- 'dead ends', implying that the intervention does not yield the expected integration, but rather puts participants temporarily or indefinitely on a route outside the regular labour market (e.g. initial training which is not matched with a subsequent, more advanced training provision; local employment initiatives focused on segments of the labour or product market for which there is no or insufficient demand; poorly managed projects);
- 'carousels', i.e. measures aiming at immediate short-term results, actually resulting in backsliding of participants into their original situa-

tion (e.g. temporary employment of MIG-receivers, just enough to make them eligible for unemployment benefits and shifting the responsibility for reintegration to a different administration; 'training mills' where participants are kept busy with little prospect of progression or transition to work);
- 'stigma effects' resulting either from the exposing of hidden handicaps (e.g. wage subsidies for MIG-recipients) or from mandatory participation in provisions with a poor reputation among employers (e.g. some compulsory training programmes; joint employment of different socially excluded groups, which creates an image of multiplication of handicaps - see the example of hard-to-place unemployed sent to sheltered workshops for disabled people).

Although the evidence about the reduced effectiveness of these types of provisions is not always straightforward nor unambiguous, a number of evaluation studies have pointed in a more or less rigorous way to low or even negative effects for the participants. More importantly, they suggest ways to avoid these pitfalls, or at least to improve the efficiency of the provisions under study.

Dead ends and carousels should be avoided by a systematic application of the 'routing' principle: at the macro- and meso-level, policies and provisions should be designed in a consistent order, without being too rigid, so that participants should always know where to go at the outcome of a project (if possible with a choice between different alternatives). The Danish labour market policy is a fairly good example of coherent policy design, even if it has certain drawbacks. At the micro-level, especially for the most disadvantaged, individual action plans should be sketched out, tailored to the needs of every job-seeker, with intermediate steps and eventually always leading into the regular labour market. Both the policies/provisions and the individual action plans should be regularly evaluated according to precise criteria, and if necessary, adapted or (for provisions, in extreme cases) suppressed.

As single organisations, even national employment agencies, are often not equipped to run the whole range of provisions that could respond to the diversity of needs of the unemployed, a rigorous application of the routing principle necessarily implies the development of *networks*: between administrations, public and private organisations, agencies and social partners. Admittedly, complex networks run a danger of becoming bureaucratic and difficult to manage; on the other hand, the analysis so far has revealed a number of strengths and weaknesses of every body, that justify collaboration.

- Public agencies have as main strengths, their large scale, stability, continuity and professionalism. Sometimes they have moreover the monopoly of certification, and the exclusive right to give an official statute and allowance to participants. However, their vocation is mostly to serve all citizens, so that their services are almost naturally tailored to the needs of the average job-seeker; they tend either to exclude or to be unable to reach the most vulnerable groups; and their organisation is unavoidably rigid, which does not enable them to develop flexible and holistic services.
- Private non-profit operators are complementary in that they can target more explicitly on the most excluded job-seekers, through less conditional access rules as well as a flexible organisation. But their innovative capacity is hampered by financial constraints, and this sometimes weighs heavily on their staffing and professionalism. Hence, public-private partnerships should greatly improve the effectiveness of policies in favour of the poor.
- The involvement of employers as a third partner may imply a danger of increased creaming off of candidates, as they are used to select the best applicants for jobs. Apart from this danger, their commitment can be most valuable, in the first place, because they are the indirect users of all services developed for job-seekers. They should at least bring in their expertise relating to the needs of the labour market. At the same time, as was already stressed in the previous chapter, when employers are involved in provisions for disadvantaged groups in an early stage, they may get more 'accustomed' to the target groups, share the social ambitions of initiators, assess the progress made by participants during a project, and thus get over their possible prejudices against them.
- Further (this point is perhaps insufficiently elaborated above) trade unions are an important partner because of their global view on the labour market situation, and because they have the reflex of defending the equal rights of individual workers and participants. Their commitment should be a guarantee against the temptation to create inferior statutes and side-tracks. Indirectly, the day-to-day involvement of trade unions in reinsertion provisions for socially excluded job-seekers will certainly improve the solidarity between workers and the jobless, between the 'insiders' and 'outsiders'.
- Last but not least, the partnerships should include the organisations representing the target groups (organisations of unemployed, NGO's) in order to translate the needs of (potential) participants and to ensure matching of measures and provisions with these needs.

In short, the remedy for segmentation, side-tracks, dead-ends and carousels is a coherent approach, based on a dynamic concept of (re)integration into the labour market, on individual or group trajectories, and on strong partnerships between the five mentioned parties.

A last conclusion relates to the problem of *stigmatisation*: this can be avoided by: (a) less mandatory programmes (so that participants are more motivated); (b) not too narrowly defining the target groups (e.g. people with 5 years of unemployment run a greater risk of stigmatisation when included in a separate programme, compared to a programme for all LTU); and (c) not mixing groups with different 'handicaps'.

Notes

1   YMCA = Young Mens Christian Association.

7 Deadweight, substitution and competition between target groups[1]

7.1 Introduction

Whereas the previous chapter dealt with the direct effects of policies for the beneficiaries, the present chapter tackles problems relating to side-effects for other groups, and for the community as a whole.

In the economic literature on employment policy two kinds of macro-economic side-effects are often mentioned together: 'deadweight' and 'substitution' effects.
- Deadweight effects relate to the fact that the jobs filled by beneficiaries of policy measures are not always 'extra' jobs created by these measures. In other words, in the absence of the measures these jobs would perhaps have been created as well, e.g. simply due to an increase in demand.
- Substitution: independently of the net number of jobs created through a measure, the mere fact of favouring one particular group might improve its (re)employment probability, but to some extent at the expense of other groups.

In the context of this report, we will not review the whole literature on deadweight and substitution as such, but concentrate, on the one hand, on the case of measures for disadvantaged groups, and on the other hand, on special cases of 'perverse substitution' within and between target groups.

7.2 Deadweight and substitution in targeted labour market programmes

7.2.1 Deadweight

As mentioned above, deadweight effects imply that part of the job creation through a policy intervention is 'spurious' and would have taken place anyhow, e.g. simply due to an increase in demand. Or in some cases the beneficiaries merely fill jobs that were previously occupied by regular workers, who retired. This was the case, for example, with part of the French 'contrats emploi-solidarité': since 1992, the contrats emploi-solidarité (CES) have become the main instrument for the labour market reintegration of disadvantaged adults. In the context of the 'Objectif 900 000' plan, long-term unemployed and MIG-recipients were given priority (and among them, LTU aged over 50, disabled people, and individuals with more than 3 years of unemployment). During the same year, about 600 000 (half-time) CES-contracts have been signed, an increase of 142 000 compared to the previous year. The will to give priority to the most disadvantaged has been reinforced by the introduction of so-called 'consolidated jobs', i.e. CES-contracts prolonged for a period of five years subsidized through tax exemptions.

On the other hand, the extension of the CES-programme accounted for more than the totality of the net job creation in the non-profit sector in 1992. Although this does not prove that an equivalent number of regular jobs would have been created in the absence of the CES-programme, one can assume that many cheap CES-contracts replace regular employment.

At the same time, for budgetary reasons, it has also been decided to cut down the number of civil servants by not filling vacancies created following retirements (about 30,000 full-time equivalents just in the first year).

The mere existence of deadweight losses in a particular programme does not imply that the programme is useless: one should just keep in mind that the net impact of the programme could be lower than what is observed in administrative data on numbers of beneficiaries.

Note that deadweight losses can be minimised through an appropriate design of the measures: in the literature on wage subsidies, for example, several authors (Layard and Nickell, 1980; Holmlund, 1980; Chiarella and Steinherr, 1982) have demonstrated that marginal wage subsidies are more effective than average subsidies. Marginal wage subsidies imply that only newly recruited workers are subsidised, instead of all workers including those who were already employed. Steinherr and Van Haeperen (1985) show also that the subsidy should not exceed the average government expenditure per unemployed (unemployment benefit plus foregone tax and social security receipts).

Selective measures targeted at disadvantaged groups are also thought to cause relatively less deadweight losses than general measures for four reasons (OECD, 1982; Bassi and Ashenfelter, 1986; OECD, 1993):
- the measures will automatically concern the more labour-intensive sectors of the economy, where more low-qualified workers are employed;
- the effect of the measures on the average wage cost will be relatively stronger, since wages of these groups are lower;
- the consumption propensity of low-wage earners is relatively higher, which may induce stronger multiplier effects; and
- employers are relatively less inclined to recruit disadvantaged workers without extra incentives, as compared to highly productive workers.

Deadweight effects are extremely difficult to estimate empirically. Estimates can be made either via macro-econometric studies that include - besides the number of beneficiaries of the programmes concerned - all other relevant context variables (growth of GDP, wages, flows of vacancies, ...), or via surveys among employers. Although the latter are less sophisticated from the theoretical and methodological point of view, they sometimes yield more reliable results. As mentioned in the introduction, we do not intend to review the whole empirical literature about deadweight here; we prefer to focus on the most relevant and recent studies on selective measures for disadvantaged groups in Europe. A noteworthy example is the study by Ameels, Lopez-Novella and Van der Linden (1994) who interviewed a stratified sample of 400 employers, selected on the basis of their recent experience with labour market measures for disadvantaged groups (LTU, poorly qualified youngsters, MIG-claimants, women re-entering the labour market, and handicapped persons). They found deadweight effects of 54-58% for wage subsidies, and of 38-49% for training measures. The lower estimate for training appears to be consistent with other studies (Bassi and Ashenfelter, 1986; OECD, 1993). Bushell (1986) evaluated a British scheme of wage subsidies to employers conditional upon the recruitment of LTU: he estimated the deadweight effect at 63%. de Koning (1991) measured an effect of barely 40% in a similar Dutch scheme, by means of econometric analysis. A sub-programme of the Dutch scheme, targeted at very long term unemployed and ethnic minorities, was even found to have no deadweight at all (de Koning, 1992). Wood and Hamilton (1989) found 69% deadweight in a study on Jobstart, a wage subsidy paid to the LTU for accepting a job within 3 months. As concerns direct employment schemes, few comparable figures are available as evaluation techniques are different; however, some studies suggest that they are effective in terms of net job creation, sometimes even more than training or wage subsidies, if at least they are targeted at the structurally unemployed (Eriksson, 1991; Bellman and Lehman, 1990). De Munnik (1992) reports a deadweight effect of only 15% in the Dutch 'labour pools' (banenpools), whereas PACEC (1992) estimates that 2/3 of the jobs created in the UK's Inner cities task force initiatives' are not really new.

7.2.2 Substitution

Independently of the net number of jobs created through a measure, the mere fact of favouring one particular group might well improve its (re-)employment probability, but to some extent at the expense of other groups.[2] E.g. recruitment subsidies in favour of the long-term unemployed can have negative effects on the employment probabilities of the short-term unemployed.

The effects of this type of substitution depend partly on the employers' (more or less subjective) appreciation of the relative productivity of different categories of job-seekers, on the strength of the incentives offered, and on the relative size of the competing groups (if the disadvantaged group favoured through a particular labour market programme constitutes only a small minority, then the danger of substitution will be less acute). In some cases, the substitution effect may even be positive, i.e. measures targeted at one group may have positive side effects for other groups. This occurs when the two types of labour under consideration are not competing against each other, but are instead complementary.[3]

The phenomenon of substitution is relatively well-known among theorists and policy makers. Estimates range from 9% for targeted training programmes (Ameels e.a., 1993) to over 80% for selective wage subsidies (de Koning e.a., 1992). Sometimes substitution is admitted to be the explicit objective of an employment programme, which implies that the only aim is to redistribute employment probabilities from 'average' job-seekers to more disadvantaged groups; and that no net job creation is expected at all. The net benefit of such programmes can still turn out positive if their cost is very moderate (e.g. with quota systems, when employers are simply obliged to recruit job-seekers from particular target groups without any form of compensation; or with jobclubs, where weaker groups are trained in assertive job search methods). The balance can also remain positive if the measures under consideration merely redistribute employment chances between groups so as to reduce the average future risk of unemployment. For example, Hui and Trivedi (1986) argue that shifting vacancies from the short-term unemployed towards the LTU is effective when there is 'negative duration dependence', i.e. when the probability of leaving unemployment diminishes with increasing unemployment duration.

The argument above is often raised in the context of wage subsidies or direct employment programmes, but it holds for training as well. Indeed, the growing discussion about the relative (in)effectiveness of training policies in the fight against unemployment relates to a large extent to substitution effects. In a segmented labour market with general disequilibrium, the most educated groups try to escape from unemployment by accepting jobs at lower levels of qualification, thus crowding out their less educated competitors, who in turn take on jobs at still lower levels, etc. The poor, situated at the bottom of the educational ladder, thus bear the burden of unemployment of the rest of the society. In this context, training policies do nothing but redistribute employment probabilities between social groups, and therefore at the macro-level their contribution to the productivity of the labour force is being called into question (see the debate about over-education).

7.3 Substitution within or between disadvantaged groups

7.3.1 Substitution within target groups

Deadweight and substitution effects may be considered unavoidable side effects of targeted labour market policies. As long as deadweight does not approach 100%, or as long as more disadvantaged groups are substituted for less disadvantaged ones, one would consider them as 'leaks' rather than 'perverse' effects.

Substitution effects become genuinely 'perverse' when they distort the employment probabilities at the expense of (some) disadvantaged job-seekers. This may happen within one single target group or between target groups. To explain the phenomenon of substitution within a target group, let us consider a simplified case: suppose that a

---

new job search assistance scheme is targeted at the LTU, but that, due to budget constraints, current resources are merely reallocated to assist half of the target group (selected at random) more intensively, instead of serving the whole population in a usual way. In this setting it can reasonably be expected that the flow of vacancies to the LTU remains unchanged. A micro-economic impact study, comparing the outflow probabilities of the treatment group with the control group, may find substantial effects of the scheme for the beneficiaries, although it is obvious from the setting that the employment probabilities were merely redistributed within the group of LTU: beneficiaries have improved their position, whereas the position of non-participants from the same target group has worsened. Although our example is extreme and artificial, it illustrates a case of perverse substitution that has long been disregarded in evaluation research. Many American evaluation studies, claiming to be more reliable because they were based on experimental designs,[4] have failed to take this kind of effect into account.

To our knowledge, the concept of substitution within target groups has been recognised but never measured in practice. Anyhow, its existence calls for caution in evaluation techniques: erroneous conclusions such as illustrated above can be avoided by measuring the (aggregate) impact of targeted measures for the target group as a whole, rather than for the participants alone.

7.3.2 Substitution between target groups

In some countries such a multitude of programmes is set up for different target groups considered as 'disadvantaged', that in the end these disadvantaged groups really compete against each other in the job market. Suppose that the long-term unemployed are 'sold off' at the same time as migrant workers, women re-entering the labour market, young people, low-qualified job-seekers, and so on. In such cases the substitution effects take place partly between disadvantaged groups mutually. The danger of uncontrolled competition between priority groups increases when employment policy is more decentralised and less coordinated (e.g. when federal measures interfere with regional policies).

One example of such competition between target groups concerns school leavers and MIG-recipients in Denmark. Both categories are often treated equally in labour market measures designed for the 'uninsured unemployed', although the two groups are not really comparable and have different needs. For example, school leavers are in general more educated: education allowances may be less useful for them, as compared to MIG-recipients. However there is evidence about young students misusing the 'education allowance scheme' for people on social welfare, so that the real target group is 'crowded out' of the system.

7.4 Reverse substitution

The worst situation occurs, of course, when the poorest are given less priority than less disadvantaged groups: in this case employment opportunities are diverted from those at the end of the queue towards more privileged groups, and poverty actually increases. To illustrate the real danger of such effects, consider the discussion about 'preventive' versus 'curative' policies vis-à-vis long-term unemployment. In a number of EC-countries active guidance plans have been launched in order to prevent people from slipping into long-term unemployment; these plans include extra mediation and training efforts, and in some cases wage subsidies as well. Because of budgetary constraints, the period in which the unemployed are given extra assistance is limited to a fixed number of months, which means that afterwards, the efforts of the employment agencies diminish again. The fear is that the concentration of mediation and training efforts on a critical period before long-term unemployment sets in, might actually lower the outflow probability from unemployment for those who have already crossed that threshold.

The problem is particularly topical in Belgium, where the regional government of Flanders has taken several measures in favour of the most disadvantaged groups, whereas the federal government has focused its strategy on preventive measures. The policies are obviously complementary, but to some extent also contradictory. For example, the Flemish 'Weer-Werk-Actie' ('back to work' action) aims to reactivate the long-term unemployed on a voluntary basis through a combination of counselling, training and work experience measures. The federal 'Guidance plan' interferes to some extent with this scheme by providing (compulsory) extra assistance to the 'almost LTU', including counselling, training and wage subsidies. In 1993, in the context of very sluggish economic growth and upsurging youth unemployment, together with the abolition of military service, the federal government launched a Youth Recruitment Plan (YRP) with wage subsidies for youngsters after 6 months of unemployment. These wage subsidies are nearly unconditional and much more attractive than the existing recruitment incentives for LTU. Whereas the Youth Recruitment Plan has had an unexpected success, labour market analysts fear that resources and opportunities are, to some extent, diverted away from the hard core of the unemployed. Since the start of the YRP, within 6 months, the share of vacancies reserved exclusively for youngsters has risen from 6 to 36% (Holderbeke, 1994). Moreover, some of the most disadvantaged among the unemployed youngsters, those who are not entitled to unemployment benefits, have no access to the YRP; even young LTU who are entitled to benefits and who had the opportunity to get some work experience in the Weer-Werk action, are (temporarily) excluded from the plan. Criticisms of these inconsistencies have recently persuaded the Minister of Employment of the need to harmonise different types of wage subsidies.

A danger of reverse substitution has also been noticed in some northern EC-member states, with ESF-interventions focused on youngsters and the LTU. At the overall EC-level, it must be acknowledged that the problems of youth unemployment and LTU are both acute, although indeed it is very difficult to weigh the relative disadvantages of both target groups against each other in an objective way. Yet, the relative position of youngsters differs widely from country to country, ranging from extremely high youth unemployment rates in Spain (37%) to barely 5% in Germany (figures for May 1993 - CEC, 1993). During the period 1990-1992, as the ESF-interventions targeted at youngsters (objective 4) exceeded those for LTU (objective 3), this resulted in a strong comparative advantage for youngsters, with a real danger of reverse substitution at the expense of LTU. This danger was accentuated by the fact that the relatively well-educated young unemployed are more easily reached by policy measures than the LTU, who are often discouraged by previous failures and poor employment expectations (see chapter 4). As the budgets for objective 4 were exhausted more quickly than those for objective 3, a tendency to shift budgets from LTU to youngsters was observed in some countries. Fortunately, the ESF drew its lessons from this experience: for the next period 1994-1999, both objectives are merged into a new 'objective 3' and it has been decided that each member state can negotiate the budgetary priorities according to its own internal distribution of unemployment risks. Of course, it remains an open question whether member states will make more rational choices about the allocation of budgets to different priority groups.

7.5 Conclusions and policy implications

From the discussion in this chapter it must be obvious that selective labour market measures have important side effects: not only is there a huge difference between gross and net effects, but a substantial redistribution of employment opportunities may take place within and between different priority groups.

The following policy recommendations can be derived from the analysis.

1. First of all, substitution and deadweight effects are so important quantitatively, that any rigorous evaluation of a labour market programme (be it a training, wage subsidy, counselling, or a direct employment programme) should include estimates of these side effects. The absence of such estimates may completely distort the picture of the programme's effectiveness. Specific attention should be given to possible 'within-group' substitution and 'reverse substitution', which have been largely neglected in research so far.

2. More precisely targeted policies appear to have less deadweight and substitution effects, and thus show a greater net effectiveness. However, this argument in favour of narrowly targeted measures should be weighted against the risk of stigma effects discussed in the previous chapter.

3. The examples of competition between target groups discussed in section 3 prove the need to establish a clear, officially approved hierarchy of priority groups, based on objective criteria such as the relative risks of unemplo[5]yment duration and on multidimensional analyses of disadvantages, in order to avoid contradictory priorities in employment policies and an inflation of target groups.

Notes

[1] With thanks to Christel Claeys (HIVA) for useful references.

[2] A specific type of substitution occurs when employers recruiting job seekers through subsidies improve their competitive position so strongly that, through competition, they force other firms out of the market, so that existing jobs are destroyed (displacement effect). However, from a theoretical point of view this effect

is completely analogous with substitution between groups of job seekers when new jobs are created.

3 The argument is theoretically underpinned in the following argument. Let L1 represent the employment of a disadvantaged group at the company level, whereas L2 represents the employment of other workers. The convex curves are isoquants and the downward sloped straight lines are the 'isocost-curves. Before government intervention, the employer's optimal allocation of L1 and L2 is reflected in point A, at which L1A and L2A are employed. The introduction of a wage cost subsidy for L1 makes the isocost curve shift outwards, yielding a new equilibrium at B, which implies a recruitment of extra workers from L1 in both figures. The effect on L2 differs in the left and right figures, however, depending on the relation between L1 and L2. The smooth isoquants at the left side mean that both types of labour are highly substitutable, so that the improvement of the position of L1 goes in pair with a loss for L2. At the right hand side, on the contrary, L1 and L2 are rather complementary, and indeed the employment of L2 improves after the introduction of the wage subsidy.

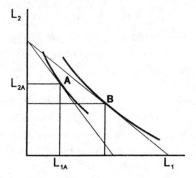 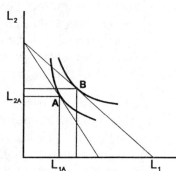

4 Note that substitution within a target group may occur irrespectively of the experimental or non-experimental design of a scheme.

8 Summary and conclusions: Towards more effective labour market policies for disadvantaged groups

The mission of this research project was to lay open contradictions and perverse effects in social policies - and more precisely, labour market policies - towards the poor. While fulfilling this mission, the research team became aware of the danger that the findings could be interpreted in very different ways. For example, one might conclude that the policies discussed in the report are so biased and ineffective, that it would not be worthwhile to pursue them: the result would be the suppression of lots of well-intended efforts, and very probably, a further exclusion of the poor (and other disadvantaged groups) from labour market participation. As this is obviously not the intention of the present report, we decided to point at examples of good practice and instances of policies being changed in the light of experience, to eliminate problems, wherever possible, and to close every chapter with a number of recommendations for the improvement of these policies.

In this final chapter, an attempt is made to draw together the main conclusions of the various chapters into a coherent set of policy recommendations, addressed to national and local authorities as well as the European Commission. These conclusions will be rearranged in the following order: design, targeting, operation, and outcome. We close the chapter with a comment on the consistency between targeted and general labour market policy.

8.1 Design

1. Special measures may be necessary to reach the most excluded groups and to respond to their particular needs. Thus for example, temporary subsidised employment in 'social economy'-initiatives may be an adequate alternative for those who are rather reluctant to undertake training; long training trajectories with a sufficient remuneration of participants are necessary to motivate those with acute financial problems to engage in initial training; a judicious use of selective marginal wage subsidies, linked with in-service guidance and counselling may help overcome employers' prejudices against very disadvantaged groups ...

   The existing evidence on the particular needs of the most excluded groups relating to labour market reintegration is very scarce. Labour market authorities should invest more in these kinds of studies.

2. Special measures should never be conceived as 'side-tracks'. They should always be integrated in a trajectory, written down in an individual action plan that stipulates all steps to be taken, with intermediate evaluation (and eventual revision), and with integration into the regular labour market as the ultimate goal.

3. As poverty is a multidimensional problem, labour market measures for the poor should be embedded in a holistic approach, including elements of social assistance, guidance and counselling, training, child care and so on.

4. Mandatory programmes may be seen in some circumstances as useful measures, but they should be avoided as a rule, as they cause demotivation of participants and stigma effects. The sanctions involved when 'beneficiaries' do not comply with the rules, or simply the lack of sufficient and adequate supply tend to result in the opposite of (re)integration.

   A good equilibrium between compulsion and efficient help can be reached by offering different options and outcome guarantees to the participants (see the recent reform of the Danish job offer scheme).

8.2 Targeting and accessibility

1. Before engaging in specific measures for separate groups, all existing forms of discrimination should be abolished. One of the basic principles of every labour market policy should be the right of every person at active age to participate in the labour market and to have access to all existing services for job-seekers.
   Defining some groups of the population a priori as being 'out of the labour force' (single parents, older unemployed, disabled persons, ...) should be regarded as a hidden form of discrimination.
   Limiting access to labour market programmes to job-seekers entitled to unemployment insurance benefits is even worse, a direct form of social exclusion.

2. Registration as a job-seeker should be facilitated, e.g. through automatic registration of some categories of social security recipients. Automatic deletion from the register for administrative reasons should be avoided.

3. Positive discrimination in favour of disadvantaged groups (e.g. LTU) can be useful in order to counteract the eternal danger of creaming off in 'mainstream' services. However, positive discrimination itself can be dangerous in several respects: (a) overlooking equally disadvantaged groups that are ipso facto excluded from the measure and whose competitive position worsens as a consequence of the measure; (b) increased complexity of measures for employers; (c) potential stigma effects of too narrowly targeted provisions.
   Perverse substitution effects (i.e. giving more help to less disadvantaged groups) should be avoided by establishing a clear, officially approved hierarchy of priority groups, based on objective criteria such as outflow probabilities from unemployment, multiple deprivation and so on.

4. Guaranteed services are a better means to ensure a minimum of equity in the delivery of services to the unemployed. They are a concrete way to realise the 'right to labour', and a necessary counterpart to compulsion.
   In some provisions (e.g. training programmes, recruitment subsidies) quota systems for particular target groups can also be used as an alternative to separate provisions.

---

5. Mixing target groups with different handicaps (e.g. disabled and hard-to-place unemployed) in single measures may cause increased stigmatisation and should therefore be avoided.

8.3 Operation

1. The socially excluded deserve well-managed services for their reintegration into the labour market. Some well-intended local initiatives (training as well as employment projects) suffer from a poor management: they can be improved by the establishment of adequate quality criteria for their approval and funding, and/or by providing management advice services.

2. Setting up partnerships and networks is an important element for a successful implementation of the 'routing' principle, as no single operator is able to offer the complete range of services that may be useful for combating exclusion from the labour market. Five (types of) partners were indentified in chapter 6, each with its strengths and weaknesses: public agencies, private organisations, employers, trade unions, and organisations representing the target groups.

3. The funding of private, local provisions needs to be made more adequate and secure, in order to allow for the development of professional and stable services. In the context of operational programmes co-financed by the ESF, the lack of long-term guarantees for small NGO-projects and the delays for payment caused by the different hierarchical stages in administrative procedures constitute a serious handicap, that could be overcome by prefinancing and longer-term agreements.

4. The injudicious use of output-related funding may turn out very harmful for the most disadvantaged groups and may even be quite inefficient from a social cost-benefit point of view (see 8.4, point 2). It seems preferable to base funding on the extent and characteristics of the target group and on criteria related to the quality of the services delivered.

8.4 Outcomes and evaluation

1. Our whole report has demonstrated the need for a continuous and rigorous evaluation of labour market policies and provisions, by pointing at examples of inefficiencies and perverse effects.

2. The short-term placement ratio (x months after participation in a programme) is a fairly simple, but socially and economically biased evaluation criterion: socially, as it tends to show better results for programmes geared towards stronger groups, and thus to reinforce creaming off mechanisms; economically, because it does not account for the long-term effects of policies.
   A more balanced evaluation of employment effects would be based (a) on 'differential' rather than absolute placement ratios (i.e. compared to a reference group of non-beneficiaries with similar characteristics); (b) on longer-term analyses (the long-term benefit of reintegrating disadvantaged individuals is expected to be greater than for the average unemployed).

3. Besides merely quantitative employment effects, one should take account of aspects like equality of access, the quality of the obtained jobs (contract terms, stability of employment, concurrence between training and job, perspectives of the sector, ...), and psychological and social effects.

4. Furthermore, one must not forget the (possibly substantial) side effects of targeted labour market policies on non-participants. In our study, we focused on negative side effects for equally or more disadvantaged groups rather than the 'classic' dead-weight and substitution effects.
   'Within-group' substitution occurs in some cases when a policy measure has a limited coverage and actually drains services and opportunities away from equally disadvantaged individuals in favour of beneficiaries. It can be overcome by providing for a sufficient capacity to cover the whole target group.
   'Reverse substitution' means that stronger measures are taken in favour of less excluded groups (e.g. youngsters), thereby reinforcing the exclusion of the less privileged (e.g. LTU, MIG-receivers). It can be avoided by establishing a clear hierarchy of priority groups (see section 8.2, point 3).

---

5. The fear for substitution in general must not be exaggerated, however. Selective labour market policies generally aim at a redistribution of opportunities rather than at large-scale job creation. However meaningful the 'additionality' criterion included in many programmes may be, it should not give way to 'side-track' provisions, which in the long run cut off reinsertion processes.

Similarly, the intention to avoid dead-weight and substitution through a more narrow targeting of measures should be weighed against the drawback of possible stigma effects.

The examples of dead-weight and different types of substitution elaborated in the text (one of them relating to ESF-interventions) confirm the need to evaluate policies in favour of disadvantaged groups against a broader macro-economic and social background.

8.5 Consistency between targeted and general labour market policies

This brings us back to one of the key issues of chapter 2, namely, the conflict between the fight against social exclusion on one hand, and the growing dualisation of European societies on the other. Although the macro-economic context of the labour market was not the focus of this study, it appeared unavoidable to devote some comments to this fundamental conflict.

Even if there were a consensus about the statement that the growing unemployment, dualisation and poverty in Europe are triggered by external shocks (oil shocks, socio-demographic shifts), much less agreement would be reached about the unavoidability of their persistence, as well as the strategies to combat them.

Economic theory and policy seem to have lost their problem-solving power. From a purely economic point of view, everybody would agree that unemployment is to be interpreted as an excess supply in labour markets. After the failure of demand-boosting and supply-reducing policies in the 1970s and 1980s, the present strategy ('active labour market policies') seems to be focused on the victims themselves: supply is stimulated, flexibilised, put under pressure in order to control wage pressures and inflation, but who believes that this will bring us back to full employment ? Some economists would argue that increased supply of commodities, including labour, can stimulate demand; the reality of the past 20 years appears not to support this thesis. And everybody knows that neither economic growth, nor 'more Europe' - however desirable they both may be - will be the ultimate answers.

From a social point of view, active labour market policies - if they are well designed and targeted - redistribute *probabilities* of employment, but are not really increasing employment for all.

It appears to us that this contradiction can only be overcome by a general redistribution of labour and income, which is obviously not a simple strategy because it requires a new social consensus, a new equilibrium of power, a greater solidarity.

Appendix 1

The LIS-database and its use to determine the labour market situation of the poor in Europe

Table A1 gives an overview of the various databases in LIS which were used for our analysis. Some surveys are weighted in order to make them representative for the country to which they apply.

Table A1

Country	Year	Survey Name	Weights
GER	1984	Das sozio-ökonomische Panel (Welle 1/Welle 2)	Yes
IT	1986	Indagine Campionaria sui Bilanci Delle Famiglie	No
NL	1987	Aanvullend Voorzieningen Onderzoek	Yes
UK	1986	The Family Expenditure Survey	No
LUX	1985	Panel Socio-Economique "Liewen zu Letzeburg"	No
BEL	1985	Socio-Economic Surveys of the Centre for Social Policy	
DK (not in LIS)	1992	The Law model System (Lovmodel)	

The poverty threshold was derived making use of the disposable household income concept as defined by LIS. The equivalence scale assigns value 1 to the first adult, value 0.7 to each additional adult and value 0.5 to each child. Household members who are less than 18 years old are statistically treated as children. For each country the median of disposable equivalent income, weighted by the number of household members and weighted by the appropriate household type weight (if present) was computed. Households whose disposable equivalent income is smaller than 50% of this median, are called poor. This procedure amounts to the poverty shares given in table A2. Obviously, this poverty threshold tells more about the inequality of the income distribution than about poverty, given the multi-dimensional nature of poverty. Even on a strictly financial basis, our results in table A2 below diverge from poverty rates estimated in other studies (for example, it is generally accepted that the figures for the UK are much higher than those for Denmark. Our poverty rate estimates are similar for both countries, which may indicate that the figures in table A2 are not very accurate). Unfortunately, however, we dispose of no better internationally comparable criterion so far. Once again, it should be noted that the Danish figures are strictly speaking not comparable with the figures for the other countries, since they are not derived from LIS.

Table A2
Share of poor households and persons

	LUX	GER	UK	NL	IT	BEL	DK
Share of poor households	4.12	5.45	6.74	5.60	9.26	4.36	6.7
Share of poor individuals	4.51	5.83	8.97	5.92	11.04	4.55	
Excluding households whose head is older than 65 :							
Share of poor households	4.02	5.39	8.47	6.91	9.13	4.20	7.8
Share of poor individuals	4.42	5.82	10.25	6.70	10.83	4.34	

Table 1.1 in chapter 1, section 2 gives the labour force participation shares, given the division poor/non-poor. In order to arrive at the four categories of labour force participation used in table 1.1, sometimes an aggregation was necessary. Table A3 gives the details of this aggregation.

Table A3
Different categories of labour force participation

Country	Working	Unemployed	Out of the labour force	Missing
GER	- Employed - Profes-sional soldier	- Looking or on layoff	- Not in labour force - Going to school - Manditory military service	Missing
IT	- Working - Home worker	- Unem-ployed - Looking for first job	- Non worker - Pensioner - Going to school - Housekeeping	
NL	- In labour force	- Looking for work	- Not in labour force - Going to school	Missing
UK	- Self employed - Full time employee at work - Part time employee at work	- Temporar-ily away from work	- Retired and of pension age - Retired and under pension age - Unoccupied	Missing
LUX	- Working		- Not working	
BEL	- Employed	- Unem-ployed with benefit - Unem-ployed without benefit	- Retired ever worked - Retired never worked - Sick - Disabled - Student over 15 - Military service - Housekeeper	Un-known

Appendix 2

Performance indicators of Flemish training schemes (illustration to chapters 4, 5 and 6)

Table A4 below summarises a number of performance indices of Flemish training schemes, measured in the context of the evaluation of ESF-cofinanced programmes (Nicaise e.a., 1995). Each column of the table relates to a specific training scheme and contains data on the profile of participants and on the effects after training. The columns 'NGO', 'VDAB-prevocational training', and 'TOK' (Tewerkstelling en Opleiding voor Kansarmen = Employment and Training for Disadvantaged) are the most relevant ones for the poor.

Table A4
Performance indicators of training provisions in the Flemish Community of Belgium, 1989-1990

	Ref. pop. (1)	NGO	VDAB-prevoc. tr. (2)	VDAB-second. sector	VDAB-tertiary sector	VDAB-indiv. tr. in enterpr.	Part-time adult educ.-new techn.	TOK =tr./empl. for MIG-rec.	Voc. tr. centres for handi-capped	Ap-prentice-ship for handi-capped
N° of unemployed coverage ratio (%)	± 210,000 -	1,128 0.5	2,441 1.2	8,119 3.9	8,306 4.0	3,705 1.8	± 600 (3) 0.3	118 0.06	964 0.5	
Profile (4)										
% LTU Total	60.1	90.5	87.5	59.2	59.0	23.3	17.7	72.3	> 43.0 (7)	-
1-2 years	17.0	25.9	28.7	28.1	25.8	12.9	8.8	16.9	-	-
2-5 years	18.5	29.7	27.2	21.3	25.4	7.0	7.9	24.1	-	-
+5 years	24.7	34.9	31.6	9.8	7.9	3.3	1.0	31.3	-	-
% Women	64.9	70.6	65.4	19.5	72.8	33.1	53.9	50.0	36.0	32.0
% low-qualified										
Primary educ.	49.3	32.9	51.5	33.3	4.0	28.0	3.5	36.0	25.2	10.0
Lower secondary	24.6	41.3	43.4	36.1	10.1	33.0	14.0	37.7	47.7	70.5

Table A4

Performance indicators of training provisions in the Flemish Community of Belgium, 1989-1990 (continued)

	Ref. pop. (1)	NGO	VDAB-prevoc. tr.. (2)	VDAB-second. sector	VDAB-tertiary sector	VDAB-indiv. tr. in enterpr.	Part-time adult educ. - new techn	TOK =train./ empl. for MIG-rec.	Voc. tr. centres for handi-capped	Ap-prentice-ship for handi-capped
Age										
-25 years	18.8	26.0	32.4	28.9	39.2	45.3	100.0	17.5	15.5	44.1
25-40 years	45.1	54.9	63.2	59.5	55.0	54.7	0.0	61.7	72.7	52.8
+40 years	36.0	19.1	4.4	11.6	5.7	0.0	0.0	20.8	11.8	3.1
% migrants	9.2	7.2	14.7	9.8	5.7	4.6	4.7	24.8	5.1	3.1
% min. income recipients	11.1	3.2	2.2	1.4	0.0	0.0	-	100.0	-	-
% with limited ability to work	12.0	5.8	5.1	6.3	3.6	-	-	-	100.0	100.0
Results (4)										
% dropouts										
Total	-	22.1	44.1	28.2	45.3	19.6	24.2	-	30.0	20.0
For other reasons than work	-	13.6	16.9	14.0	8.6	14.0	19.0	20.0	17.0	16.0

Table A4
Performance indicators of training provisions in the Flemish Community of Belgium, 1989-1990
(continued)

	Ref. pop. (1)	NGO	VDAB-prevoc. tr.. (2)	VDAB-second. sector	VDAB-tertiary sector	VDAB-indiv. tr. in enterpr.	Part-time adult educ.- new techn	TOK =train./ empl. for MIG-rec.	Voc. tr. centres for handi-capped	Ap-prentice-ship for handi-capped
% employed (5)										
After 3 months	-	36.2	43/21	65/43	70/45	79/39	-	36/30	62.0	68.0
After 6 months	-	40.0	43/19	65/45	72/53	79/44	51.7	38/30	58.0	69.0
After 12 months	-	36.0	47/19	70/43	69/49	78/45	-	41/24	60.0	68.0
% concurrence tr. - job										
Complete	-	20.0	17.1	41.2	29.2	64.2	-	22.5	-	-
Partial	-	26.1	19.0	18.3	41.5	11.6	-	37.5	-	-
% transition to further training										
After 3 months	-	8.1	3.7	2.8	0.7	2.8	54.4	5.0	2.0	1.0
After 6 months	-	7.5	5.1	3.5	2.9	2.8	-	4.7	1.0	1.0
After 12 months	-	5.5	2.9	2.8	4.3	0.9	-	1.7	1.0	1.0

(1) Reference population = non-working job seekers (insured or not) + minimum income recipients, Flemish Community - 1989.

(2) In principle all data w.r.t. profiles of participants are drawn from official sources and relate to the entire population of participants. For the prevocational after training courses of the VDAB, however, no administrative data are available, so that we have to rely on our own sample results.

(3) The part-time adult education courses in new technologies have 4 310 participants, among which only 14% are unemployed. The profile data relate only to unemployed participants and are drawn from our own survey (Simoens, 1993).

(4) In contrast with the profile data (that are based on administrative sources), the data on 'results' are based on our own survey. These results relate only to participants eligible for subsidisation under ESF-objectives 3 and 4: consequently, they are not representative for the whole population of participants.

(5) In columns where two placement ratios appear, the first one relates to participants and the second one to a comparison group.

(6) The exact duration of unemployment before entering a 'bridge project' is unknown.

(7) The proportion of participants eligible under objective 3 amounts to 43%; among the objective 4 population, a number of participants may be LTU as well.

Bibliography

A.T.D.-Quart-Monde, *L'impact du rapport Wresinski en France '1987-1991'*, 1991, 30 p.

Aarkrog V. e.a., UTB, *Uddannelsestilbud for langtidsledige* (UTB. Training courses for long-term unemployed persons), København: Danmarks Lærerhøjskole & Udviklingscenter for folkeoplysning og voksenundervisning, 1991.

Abou-Sada G. (ed.), *Local develeopment and strategies to combat poverty*, Commision of the European Communities-Directorate general employment, industrial relations and social affairs, 1991, 126 p.

Abou-Sada G. (ed.), *Partenaires sociaux et exclusion sociale*, Commision of the European Communities-Directorate general employment, industrial relations and social affairs, 1992, 114 p.

Abou-Sada G. (ed.), *Repertoire des projets*, Commision of the European Communities-Directorate general employment, industrial relations and social affairs, 1991, 139 p.

Abou-Sada G., *Europe against poverty*, Commission of the European Communities-Directorate general employment, industrial relations and social affairs, 1991, 48 p.

Abou-Sada G., Yeates N. (eds.), *Research problematics*, Commission of the European communities Directorate general employment, industrial relations and social affairs, 1991, 263 p.

Ameels J.-Ch., Lopez-Novella M., Van der Linden B., *Apport d'une enquête auprès de firmes à la définition de politiques favorisant l'embauche des groupes concernés par l'objectif 3*, IRES, Univ. Cath. de Louvain, 1994, 41 p.

Ameels J.-Ch., Lopez-Novella M., Van der Linden B., *Rapport final sur les effets indirects des stratégies de lutte contre le chômage*, IRES, Univ. Cath. de Louvain, 1993, 57 p.

Andersen B.R., Economic mutations and social exclusion: employment strategies, in Abou-Sada (ed., 1992).

Animation et Recherche EEIG, *SPES Database: bibliographical review on poverty and social exclusion* (2 volumes: documents in French and English), Lille, dec. 1993.

Ashton D.N. e.a., *A comparison of education and training in Canada and Britain*, 1992.

Ashton D.N., Sources of variation in Labour market segmentation: a comparison of Canadian and Britisch youth labour markets, in *Work, employment and society*, 1988, 2(1).

Aucouturier A.-L., Contribution à la mesure de l'efficacité de la politique de l'emploi, *Travail et Emploi*, 1993 (55), DARES, p. 20-30.

Baron C., Bureau M.-L., Nivolle P., Porcher P., *L'action experimentale 'contre l'exclusion, une qualification' et les practiques de gestion de la main-d'oeuvre dans les entreprises*, Centre d'études de l'emploi, Noisy Le Grand Cedes 1992, 84 p.

Basile E., Cecchi C., North and south development, growth and poverty, in Abou-Sada G. e.a. (eds.), 1991.

Bassi L., Ashenfelter O., The effect of direct job creation and training program on low-skilled workers, in Danziger S., Weinberg D. (eds.), 1986, p. 133-51.

Bauer, Vom zweiten in den ersten Arbeitsmarkt, in *Blätter der Wohlfahrtspflege*, March 1994.

Bell S.H., Is subsidized employment cost effective for welfare recipients ?, *J. Hum. Res.*, 29(1), Winter 1994, p. 42-61.

Bellman L. & Lehmann H., *Active labour market policies in Britain and Germany and long-term unemployment: an evaluation*, Paper for the EALE Conference, Lund, 1990.

Bellman L., Evaluation of measures to combat long term unemployment, in Applied Econometrics Association, *Modeling the labour market*, Proceedings of the Strasbourg Conference, Dulbea, Vol. II, p. 145-151.

Benoit-Guilbot O., Gallie D., *Chomeurs de longue durée*, Actes-Sud, Observatoire du changement social en Europe Occidentale, Poitiers, 1992, 231 p.

Bono & Sarazin, *Rapport sur le développement des entreprises d'insertion*, IGAS, 1992.

Bouquillard O., L'impossible politique de l'emploi ?, *Sociologie du Travail*, 3-4/92 and 1/93.

Bourdieu P., *Le mieux du monde*, Ed. Seuil, fév. 1993, 947 p.

Brun P., Guillot F., Viard T., *Evaluation du Crédit Formation Individualisé au regard des jeunes issus des milieux très défavorisés*, A.T.D.-Quart Monde, 1992, 77 p.

Burtless G., Are targeted wage subsidies harmfull ? Evidence from a wage voucher experiment, *Industrial and Labor relations Revieuw*, 39(1), October 1985, p. 104-118.

Bushell R., Evaluation of the Young Workers' Scheme, *Employment Gazette*, May 1986.

Cantillon B., Marx I., Proost D., Van Dam R., *Indicateurs sociaux: 1985-1992*; Centrum voor Sociaal Beleid, Univ. of Antwerp (UFSIA), 1994.

Capet C., Kervyn A., *Quelles possibilités de réinsertion professionnelle existe-t-il pour les bénéficiaires du minimex ?* CRIDIS, Brussel 1991.

Carton B. & de Crombrugghe D., L'insertion par l'économique en Europe, Bruxelles, Commission des Communautés Européennes, 1993.

Centre for Labour Market Studies, *'Evaluation Study of European Social Fund co-financed Recruitment Incentives in the UK'* University of Leicester, Leicester 1991, 56 p.

CERC, *Atouts et difficultés des allocataires du revenu minimum d'insertion*, Rapport final, Centre d'étude des revenus et des coûts, Paris 1991, 288 p.

Chérain A. and Demazière D., in Verdié M. and Sibille H., *Former pour insérer*, Syros 1992.

Chiarella C. and Steinherr A., *Marginal employment subsidies: an effective policy to generate employment*, Working Paper n° 8208, IRES, Univ. Cath. de Louvain, 37 p.

Christiansen L., *Uddannelsestilbud til arbejdsløse. En evaluering af uddannelsestilbudsordningen inden for handelsskoleområdet* (Training courses for unemployed: an evaluation of the Danish training course system), København: Danmarks Lærerhøjskole 1991.

Commission des Communautés Européennes, *La Communauté lutte contre l'exclusion sociale*, Commission des communautés européenes, Bruxelles 1992, p. 10

Commission des Communautés Européennes, *Programme d'action communautaire à moyen terme pour une intégration économique et sociale des groupes les moins favorisés*, Bulletin des Communautés européennes, 1989, 33 p.

Commission des Communautés Européennes, *Rapport final du second programme européen de lutte contre la pauvreté 1985-1989*, Commission des Communautés Européennes, Bruxelles 1991, 77 p.

Commission des Communautés Européennes, *Vers une Europe des solidarités*, Bruxelles 1992, 52 p.

Commission of the European Community, *Employment in Europe - 1993*, Commission of the European Communities, Bussels 1993.

Commission of the European Community, *European social policy options for the Union (Green paper)*, Brussels 1994.

Commission of the European Community, *Growth, competitiveness and employment (White paper)*, Brussels 1994.

Commission of the European Community, *Medium-term Community Action programme to foster the economic and social integration of the least privileged groups: transnational economic and social research programme*, Commission of the European Com., 1992, 10 p.

Commission of the European Community, *Social protection in Europe*, Brussels 1994.

Commission of the European Community, *The perception of poverty in Europe*, Brussels 1994 (forthcoming).

Commission of the European Community, *Towards a Europe of solidarity*, Commission of the European Communities, Bussels 1992, 47 p.

Communautés Européennes, Recommandation du conseil du 24 juin 1992, *Journal officiel des Communautés européennes*, 1992.

Conseil supérieur de l'action sociale, *Rapport sur le RMG*, Luxembourg, 1993.

Crook T., *The YMCA Foyer pilots: the first six months*, Employment Service - Research and evaluation report, Shiffield 1994.

Crowley-Bainton & White M., *Employing Unemployed people: How Employers Gain. Report to the Employment Service*, Policy Studies Institute, 1990.

Cutler T., Haslam C., Williams J., Williams K., *1992: the struggle for Europe*, Berg, New York 1989.

Danziger S. and Weinberg D. (eds.), *Fighting poverty: what works and what does not*, Harvard U.P. 1986, 418 p.

Dawes L., *Long-term unemployment and labour market flexibility*, Centre for Labour Market Studies, University of Leicester, 1993, 151 p.

de Koning J., Gravesteijn-Ligthelm J., 't Hoen N., Verkaik A., *Werkt de KRA ?*, Arbeidsvoorziening, Rijswijk 1992.

de Koning J., Guaranteed jobs for the young: does it work ?, in *Proceedings of the European seminar on 'Trade Unions, unemployment, and social exclusion'*, HIVA, Leuven 1994.

---

de Koning J., Koss M., Verkaik A., A quasi-experimental evaluation of the vocational training centres for adults, in *Environment and Planning, C: Government and Policy*, 9, p. 143-153.

de Koning J., Measuring the placement effects of two wage-subsidy schemes for the long-term unemployed, *Empirical Econ.*, 1993 (forthcoming).

De Munnik R., *Recent evaluation studies, Part Two*, Employment Service, Rijswijk 1992

De Vos K., Eloy M., Nicaise I., Vanheerswynghels A., *Evaluation ex-ante des politiques belges de lutte contre le chômage de longue durée co-financées par le Fonds Social Européen*, HIVA, Leuven 1991.

De Witte H., *Between optimist and withdrawn. Some preliminary results of a psycho-social typology of the long-term unemployed in Belgium*, Paper presented at the Sixth European Congress on Work and Organisational Psychology, Alicante 14-17 April 1993, 9 p.

Deleeck H., Van den Bosch K., De Lathouwer L. (eds.), *Poverty and the adequacy of social security in the EC*, Avebury, Aldershot 1992, 201 p.

Dijon X., Bodart M., Delbrouck R. et Amory C., *Promotion Emploi Formation. Formules accessibles aux chercheurs d'emploi couverts ou non par l'assurance-chômage*, FOREM/FUNDP-Namur, Centre de recherche droit et sécurité d'existence, 1992.

Eloy M. & Nicaise I., *Het opleidingsaanbod van de VDAB en 'derden' voor langdurig werklozen en jongeren: specificiteit, complementariteit en effectiviteit (The training provisions from VDAB and NGO's in favour of LTU and youngsters: specificity, complementarity and effectiveness)*, HIVA, Leuven 1993.

Employment Policy Institute, *'Making Workstart Work'* Employment Policy Institute London 1993, 6 p.

Engelund H. et al., *At yde for at nyde ?* (Contributing before benefiting ? An evaluation of the Danish Youth Allowance scheme), København: Socialforskningsinstituttet. Rapport 92: 20, 1992.

ERGO => see P.A. Cambridge Economic Consultants

Eriksson T., *The effects of labour market policies on unemployment inflow and outflow rates in Finland*, EALE-Conference, El Escorial, sept. 1991, 25 p.

Felstead A., *Funding government training schemes: mechanisms and consequences*, Leicester, Centre for Labour Market Studies, 1994.

Gaffikin F. & Morrissey M., *The new unemployed. Joblessness and poverty in the market economy*, Zed Books, London 1992.

GES, *Evaluation of the policies for the long-term unemployed in Spain (final report)*, Gabinet d'Estudis Socials, Barcelona 1991, 87 p.

Glücklich & Boulez, Verlierer sind die Benachteiligten, in *Durchblick*, January, 1993.

Godinot X., *Les travailleurs sous-prolétaires face aux mutations de l'emploi*, Ed. Science et Service-Quart Monde, 1985, 150 p.

Goodman A., Webb S., *For richer, for poorer*, Inst. for Fiscal Studies/J. Rowntree Trust, York 1994.

Grahl J. & Teague P., *1992: the big market*, Lawrence and Wishart, London 1990.

Gregersen O., *Revalidering?* (Rehabilitation?), København: Socialforskningsinstituttet. Upubliceret 1993.

Grezard, *Premières Informations*, juin 1993, n° 340.

Gueron J.M. and Pauly E., *From welfare to work*, Russell Sage Foundation, New York 1991.

Gustafsson B., Lindblom M., Poverty lines and poverty in seven european countries, Australia, Canada and the USA., *Journal of European Social Policy*, 1993, 3(1), p. 21-38.

Hausman P., *Les effects de la protection sociale dans la Communauté Européenne*, CEPS/Instead, Walferdange 1993, 44 p.

Haveman R. and Hollister R., Direct job creation: economic evaluation and lessons for the United States and Western Europe, in Björklund A. et al. (eds.), *Labour marker and unemployment insurance*, Clarendon Press, Oxford 1991, p. 5-65.

Holderbeke F., Conjunctuur en Arbeidsmarktindicatoren, *Werkgelegenheid-Arbeid-Vorming (Nieuwsbrief Steunpunt WAV)*, 1994 (1), p. 37-46.

Holmlund B., Employment subsidies and the behaviour of the firm, in Eliasson G. and Södersten J., *Business taxation, finance and firm behaviour*, Almquist and Wicksell, Stockholm 1978, p. 267-293.

Hoskins M., Maguire M., *Age as a barrier to employment. Older workers in the East Midlands*, Labour Market Studies Group, University of Leister, 1990, 85 p.

Hoskins M., Sing J., Ashton D., Job competition and the entry to work, Dept. of Econ. discussion paper, Univ. Leister.

Hui W., Trivedi P., Duration dependence, targeted employment subsidies and unemployment benefits, *J. Publ. Econ.*, 1986, 31, p. 105-129.

IED, *Contre le chômage de longue durée au Portugal*, Instituto de estudos para o desenvolvimento, Lisboa 1991, 86 p.

Ingerslev O., *Arbejde, uddannelse eller ledighed?* ('Work, education or unemployment?'), AKF-report, 1994.

James R.L., *Why can't they get jobs? The long-term unemployed and designing Employment Service interventions to help them - a literature synthesis,*

Employment Department, Psychological Services Report n° 439, Sheffield 1993.

Jensen P, Winter, Mannieke, ørberg, Thaulow I., *Measures for the LTU in Denmark*, AKF, 1991.

Jensen P. et al., *Arbejdsmarkeds-uddannelserne Evaluering af Effekten på Arbejdsløshed og Løn (Evaluation of employment and wage effects of labour market training programmes)*, Working paper n° 91-3, Centre for Labour Economics, August 1991.

Jensen P., Pedersen P., Smith N., Westergard-Nielsen N., *Measuring the effects of labour market programmes*, EALE-Conference, Warwick 1992.

Kleinman M., Piachaud D., European social policy: conceptions and choices in *Journal of European Social Policy*, 1993, 1-19.

Kongshøj Madsen P., *ATB: Bedre end sit rygte - men ikke god nok. Udkast til rapport* (Better than expected, but not good enough. An assessment of theDanish Job Offer scheme), København, januar 1992.

Labour Market Quarterly Report, Employment Department Sheffield, 20 p.

Lawlor J. & Kennedy C., 'Measures of Unemployment; the Claimant Count and the Labour Force Survey' in *The Employment Gazette*, Employment Department London 1992.

Layard R., Nickel S., Jackman R., *'Unemployment, Macroeconomic performance and the labour market'* Oxford University Press Oxford 1991, 618 p.

Layard R., Nickel S., The case for subsidizing extra jobs, Econ. J., 90, 1980, p. 51-73.

Linde P.C., *Tilfredsheden med handlings-planer blandt ledige i Ribe Amt (satisfaction with action-plans among unemployed in Ribe Rigions)*, Socialforskeningsinstituttet, 1994.

Lux B., La formation professionnelle par l'ONEM, in *Les finances publiques belges*. 6ème Congrès des économistes belges de langue française, Charleroi, CIFOP, 1984, p. 179-232.

Lynn P., *Employment Training: a survey of trainees, 1991*. Social and Community Planning Research, London 1992.

Macuire M., Green F., Wray K., *Study of urban unemployment in Nottingham. Final Report*, Labour Market Studies Group, University of Leister, 1990, 44 p.

Macuire M., Green F., Wray K., *Study of urban unemployment in Nottingham. Technical Annex*, Labour Market Studies, University of Leicester, 1990, 24 p.

Maerkedahl I., Rosdahl A. & Thaulow I., *Genveje til beskæftigelse ?* (Short-cuts to employment ? Final report on the four evaluations of the Danish Job Offer scheme) Socialforskningsinstituttets publikation 1992:14, København 1992.

Maier F., *The regulation of part-time work: a comparative study of six EC Countries, Forschngsschwerpunkt Arbeitsmarkt und Beschäftigung*, Berlin 1992, 138 p.

Maroy C., *Chômage et formation professionnelle*, Louvain-la-Neuve, CIACO/Namur, Presses Univ., 1990, 227 p.

Maroy C., Les évolutions de la formation professionnelle en Belgique francophone (1960-85). Déterminants économiques et sociaux des politiques de formation et organisation de la transition professionnelle des chômeurs, in *De l'école à l'entreprise, nouvelle donne pour la formation*, Louvain-la-Neuve, Inst. des Sc. du Travail, 1988, p. 95-119.

Ministère de la recherche et de l'espace, *Formation et apprentissage des adulter peu qualifiés*, Ministère de la recherche et de l'espace, La documentation française, 1992, 240 p.

MISEP, Basic Information Reports (on the labour market policies in the EC member states.

Murray I., Business start-up: barrier to the enterprising unemployed, *Working Brief*, May 1994, Unemployment Unit and Youthaid.

Nicaise I. et al., *Opleidings- en vormingsprojecten voor langdurig werklozen in België (Training projects for long-term unemployed in Belgium)*, HIVA, Leuven 1990, 96 p.

Nicaise I. et al., Profil de la population des chômeurs et conséquences pour l'assurance-chômage, in Alaluf M. et al. (eds.), *L'assurance-chômage dans les années nonante*, Univ. Pers, Leuven 1992, p. 89-102.

Nicaise I., *Determinants of labour earnings in Belgium: Human capital and social barriers*, EALE-conference (Eur. Assoc. of Labour Ec.), Lund (Sweden) 20-23 sept. 1990, 35 p.

Nicaise I., Douterlungne M., *Alternating education for disadvantaged youth in Flanders (Belgium): its costs and benefits for youngsters and employers*, EALE-conference, El Escorial 26-29 sept. 1991, 15 p.

Nicaise I., *Poverty and social (im)mobility*, CES-research paper, Leuven sept. 1980 (part one) en febr. 1983 (part two), 188 p.

Nicaise I., Recht op arbeid voor allen. Blauwdruk voor een langetermijnbeleid tegen dualisering van de arbeidsmarkt (Right to work for all. Blueprint of a long-term policy against dualisation of the labour market), *De Gids op Maatschappelijk Gebied*, 84(4), 1993, p. 317-346.

Nicaise I., Stradling R., *Prevocational education and training for disadvantaged youth: a framework for evaluation/Enseignement et formation pré-*

professionels pour les jeunes défavorisés: une grille d'évaluation, Nat. Foundation for Educ. Research, Slough, HIVA, Leuven 1992.

Nicaise I. et al., *Les groupes faibles face au marché de l'emploi: point de mire du Fonds social européen*. Evaluation ex-post du cadre communautaire d'appui belge 1990-92 relatif aux objectifs 3-4, rapport n° 5C (synthèse générale), HIVA, Leuven 1995.

Nicaise I., Bollens J., Dawes L., Laghaei S., Thaulou I., Verdié M., Wagner A., Pitfalls and dilemmas in labour market policies for disadvantaged groups - and how to avoid them, *Journal of European Social Policy*, 5(3), August 1995.

Nijsmans I, *De effectiviteit van ESF-projecten in het Vlaams deeltijds onderwijs: alternerend leren en brugprojecten (The effectiveness of ESF-projects in Flemish part-time education: alternating education and 'bridge projects')*, HIVA, Leuven 1993.

OECD, *Employment outlook 1992*.

OECD, *Employment outlook 1993*.

OECD, *Labour market policies for the 1990's*, OECD, Paris 1990.

OECD, *Marginal employment subsidies*, Paris 1992.

OECD, *Measures to assist long-term unemployed*. Recent experiences in some OECD Countries, OECD, Paris 1988.

Økonomiministeriet Danmark, *Lovmodel. Beretning om lovmodelrådets virksomhed og lovmodelarbejdet i 1992, lavindkomstfamilier i Danmark*, (with English summary) Copenhagen 1993.

Oppenheim C., *Poverty: the facts*, CPAG ltd., London 1993.

Otte R., Schlegel W., *Continuing education and training of the LTU in 10 member-states of the European Community*, Cedefop, 1991.

P.A. Cambridge Economic Consultants, *An action programme for the long-term unemployed: report of the first year*, Cambridge 1989.

P.A. Cambridge Economic Consultants, *An evaluation of the Government's inner cities task force initiatives*, Min. of Environment, 1992.

P.A. Cambridge Economic Consultants, *Counselling, advice and guidance*, Cambridge 1990.

P.A. Cambridge Economic Consultants, *European directory of local projects*, Cambridge 1990.

P.A. Cambridge Economic Consultants, *Evaluating long-term unemployment programmes and projects: a methodological framework*, Cambridge 1989.

P.A. Cambridge Economic Consultants, *Evaluation pack: critical questions facing policy makers*, Cambridge 1990.

P.A. Cambridge Economic Consultants, *Measures in favour of the long-term unemployed in the European Community*, Cambridge 1990.

Pacolet J. (ed.), *Social protection and the European economic and monetary union*, HIVA, EZA, Leuven, Köningswinter 1992, 77 p.

Pedersen P.J., *Persistent unemployment - aspects of the Danish experience*, Centre for Labour Market and Social Research, February 1994.

Perret B. & Rousteng G., *L'économie contre la société*, Coll. Esprit, Seuil, févr. 1993, 275 p.

Pilegaard Jensen T., Winter S., Manniche J., Ørberg P.D., *Indsatsen for langtidsledige* (Measures against unemployment. An evaluation of the Danish Job Offer scheme), København: Amternes og Kommunernes Forskningsinstitut, 1991.

Robbins D.(ed.), Laczko F., Bennington J., Breda J., *L'emploi et le marché du travail*, Programme européen de lutte contre la pauvreté, 1992, 25 p.

Robbins D., Marginalization and social exclusion in Abou-Sada G. et al. (eds.), 1991.

Room G. et al. II, *'National Policies to combat Social Exclusion - First Annual Report of the European Community Observatory'* Commision of the European Communities Brussels 1991, 43 p.

Room G. et al. II, *Second Annual Report of the European Community Observatory on national policies to combat social exclusion*, Commision of the European Communities Brussels 1992, 43 p.

Schlegel W., Langzeitarbeitslosigkeit-Was tun mit dem harten Kern ?, *Durchblick*, Junuary, 1991.

Sibille H., Verdié M., Les action d'insertion et de formation: la formation est-elle la juste résponse aux chômage de longue durée ? in *Le Chômage de longue durée*, Editions Syros 1992.

Simoens P., *Het opleidingsbeleid in het reconversiegebied Turnhout (Training policy in the context of the regional reconversion process in Turnhout)*, HIVA, Leuven 1993, 137 p.

Smeeding T., O'Higgins M., Rainwater L., *Poverty, inequality and income distribution in comparative perspective. The Luxemburg Income Study*, Harvester-Wheatsheaf, New York/London 1990, 193 p.

Smeeding T.M., Rainwater L., Rein M., Hauser R., Schaber G., Income poverty in seven countries. Initial estimates from the LIS database, uit Smeeding T.M., O'Higgins M. and Rainwater L. (eds.), 1990.

Smith D. (ed) *'Understanding the Underclass'* Policy Studies Institute, London 1992, 95 p.

Sørensen A., Equal opportunity and poverty, in Abou-Sada G. et al. (eds.), 1991.

Steinherr A., Van Haeperen B., Approche pragmatique pour une politique de plein emploi: les subventions à la création d'emplois, *Bulletin de l'IRES*, 86, Univ. Cath. de Louvain, 1986, 60 p.

Thaulow I. & Anker N., *Hvordan virker indsatsen for de ledige?* (How do
employment measures work? Evaluation of the Danish Job Offer
scheme), København: Socialforskningsinstituttet. Rapport 92: 1,
1992.

Thaulow I., *Arbejdsdeling og samarbejde* (Division of labour and cooperation between social welfare centres and employment agencies),
København: Socialforskningsinstituttet. Arbejdsnotat 1989:4, 1989.

Thaulow I., *Evaluering af ATB-lovrevisionen. Delresultater* (Evaluation of
the job offer scheme: first results), Socialforskningsinstituttets arbejdsnotat Kfbenhavn, 1991.

Thaulow I., *Kontanthjælp i praksis*. (Social assistance in practice in Denmark), København: Socialforskningsinstituttet. Rapport 90: 14, 1990.

Townsend P., *Poverty in the United Kingdom*, Hammondsworth, Pen-
guin 1979.

Valbak Aa. & Wamsler J., *Revalideringsindsatsens erhvervsmæssige effekt.*
(The employment effects of rehabilitation in Denmark), København:
Amternes og Kommunernes Forsningsinstitut, 1986.

Van de Velde V., *Wat na de sociale tewerkstelling? (What happens after social employment?)*, HIVA, Leuven 1992.

Van der Aalst M., Peters M., *De harde kern in de bijstand*, Ministerie van
Sociale Zaken en Werkgelegenheid, 1991, 114 p.

Van Meensel R., Bogaert G., *Opleiding of werkgelegenheid? Evaluatie van
7 projecten voor kansarmen (Training or employment? Evaluation of 7
projects for disadvantaged people)*, HIVA, Leuven 1992.

Van Meensel R., *Maatwerk in het OCMW (Individualised reintegration
schemes in social welfare centres)*, HIVA, Leuven 1992.

Vanhuysse J., Henkes P., Werken aan werk. Flexibele arbeidsmodellen
voor de armsten (Working for work. Flexible labour models for the
poorest), Fondation Roi Baudouin, Brussels 1992, 120 p.

Vanlerenberghe P. et al. II, *RMI: la part de l'insertion. Rapport de la
Commission nationale d'evaluation du RMI* (2 tômes), La Documentation française, 1992, 800 p.

Vanroelen C., *Beleidsverkennend onderzoek rond doorstroming in de sector
beschutte tewerkstelling*, VLAB, Hasselt 1992.

Verdié M., Sibille H., Recherche-évaluation sur la mise en oeuvre des
actions d'insertion et de formation, in *Former pour insérer*, Editions
Syros 1992.

Verdié M., *Voyage à l'intérieur du RMI*, Syros 1991.

Viveret P., *L'évaluation des politiques et des actions publiques - évaluation du Revenu minimum d'insertion*, Rapport au Premier Ministre, La Documentation Française, 1989.

Wagner A., *A comparative study of effective pre-vocational training practice*, CEPS/INSTEAD, doc. de recherche, nr. 91/13, 1991

Wagner A., *ERGO: Initiatives et projets au Grand-Duché*, CEPS/INSTEAD, 1991.

Wagner A., *Evolution d'un groupe de ménages pauvres entre 1985 et 1987*, Document PSELL nr. 11; CEPS/INSTEAD, 1989.

Wagner A., *La recherche sur la pauvreté au G-D de Luxembourg*, Document PSELL nr. 36; CEPS/INSTEAD, 1990.

Wagner A., *Les dispositifs de garantie de ressources: rapport sur le Luxembourg*, CEPS, 1992.

Wagner A., Premier bilan relatif au questionnaire Petra, CEPS/INSTEAD, 1990.

Wagner A., *Stepping out of the minimum income benefits: a survey of households losing minimum income benefits in 1990 in Luxembourg*, document de recherche PSELL n°93/18, 1993.

Westergård-Nielsen N., Effects of training: a fixed-effect model, in *Evaluating the effects of active labour market policies*, Danish Ministry of Labour, 1993.

White M., *'Against Unemployment'* Policy Studies Institute London 1991, 274 p.

White M., and Lakey J., *The Restart effect. Does active labour market policy reduce unemployment ?*, Policy Studies Institute, London 1992, 202 p.

White M., and Mcrae S., *'Young Adults and Long-Term Unemployment'* Policy Studies Institute London 1989, 289 p.

Williams F., Employment and unemployment in the European Community, in Abou-Sada G. et. al. (eds.), 1991.

Wood D., Hamilton L., *People on Jobstart*. Social and Community Planning Research, 1989.

Wouters M., Struyven L., *Kansarm op de arbeidsmarkt, kansrijk op de opleidingsmarkt ? (Poor on the labour market, rich on the training market ?)*, Koning Boudewijnstichting, Brussel 1992.

Wouters M., Van Meensel R., Nicaise I., *De TOK-projecten en hun cursisten, drie jaar later. Follow-up onderzoek van de projecten van 1989 (TOK-projects for labour market reintegration of MIG-beneficiaries, three years later. A follow-up study of the projects from 1989)*, HIVA, Leuven 1994, 71 p.

Wresinski J., *Grande pauvreté et précarité economique et sociale*, Journal Officiel France 1987.

Wuhl S., *Les exclus face à l'emploi*, Syros-Alternatives, 1992.

Zeuthen H., *Rapport fra udredningsudvalget om arbejdsmarkedets struktur-problemer* (Report from the Commission on structural problems of the labour market), København: Finansministeriet, 1992.

-, *Contre l'exclusion: quels parcours d'insertion professionelle et de qualification ?*, Reure Quart Monde, Dossier et documents no 3, 1992, 150 p.

-, *Evaluating the effects of active labour market policies*, Danish Ministry of Labour, 1993.

-, *Evaluation des stages de réinsertion en alternance.*

-, *Poverty 3 - the 39 projects.*

-, *The Luxemburg Income Study. LIS information guide (revised)*, CEPS/INSTEAD, March 1991, 21 p.